Taste of Home

THE new potluck

the best recipes for today's "bring-a-dish" meals

Reader's Digest

The Reader's Digest Association, Inc.
Pleasantville, New York/Montreal

A TASTE OF HOME/READER'S DIGEST BOOK
© 2006 Reiman Media Group, Inc.
5400 S. 60th St., Greendale, WI 53129

Editor:	Michelle Bretl
Art Director:	Nicholas Mork
Executive Editor, Books:	Heidi Reuter Lloyd
Senior Editor, Retail Books:	Jennifer Olski
Proofreader:	Julie Blume Benedict
Graphic Art Associates:	Ellen Lloyd
	Catherine Fletcher
Editorial Assistant:	Barb Czysz
Food Editor:	Janaan Cunningham
Associate Food Editors:	Coleen Martin
	Diane Werner
Assistant Food Editor:	Karen Scales
Senior Recipe Editor:	Sue A. Jurack
Recipe Editors:	Janet Briggs
	Mary King
Senior Test Kitchen Home Economists:	Peggy Fleming RD
	Pat Schmeling
	Wendy Stenman
	Amy Thieding RD
Test Kitchen Home Economists:	Tina Johnson
	Ann Liebergen
	Annie Rose
Test Kitchen Assistants:	Rita Krajcir
	Kris Lehman
	Sue Megonigle
	Megan Taylor
Senior Food Photographer:	Rob Hagen
Food Photographers:	Dan Roberts
	Jim Wieland
Associate Photographer:	Lori Foy
Set Stylists:	Stephanie Marchese
	Sue Myers
	Jennifer Bradley Vent
Associate Set Stylist:	Melissa Haberman
Food Stylists:	Sarah Thompson
	Joylyn Trickel
Photo Studio Coordinator:	Suzanne Kern
Creative Director:	Ardyth Cope
Senior Vice President, Editor in Chief:	Catherine Cassidy
President:	Barbara Newton
Founder:	Roy Reiman

Pictured on front cover: Chicken Asparagus Pasta Supper (recipe on p. 27)

International Standard Book Number: 0-89821-458-0
Library of Congress Control Number: 2005931970

For other Taste of Home books and products, visit www.tasteofhome.com
For more Reader's Digest products and information, visit our website
www.rd.com (in the United States)
www.rd.ca (in Canada)
Printed in China
3 5 7 9 10 8 6 4 2

table of contents

THE new potluck

With 172 exciting main dishes, salads, desserts and more in this brand-new recipe collection, your potluck cooking will never be the same!

POTLUCK MEALS HAVE BEEN A TRADITION IN FAMILIES AND COMMUNITIES FOR generations. But who says they have to be routine?

You'll bring excitement, fun and sensational food to every "bring-a-dish" meal when you rely on *Taste of Home's The New Potluck*. Inside this one-of-a-kind cookbook, you'll find a wide variety of potluck-size recipes—172 of them—all deliciously different and guaranteed to wow the crowd.

Family gatherings...school events...church activities...get-togethers with friends...no matter what kind of potluck you have, this unique cookbook gives you dozens of fresh-approach recipes they'll love. And because these irresistible dishes are also easy to prepare, they're perfect for today's on-the-go lifestyles.

Choose from eye-catching main dishes, salads, appetizers, soups, cakes, bars and much more—all shown in gorgeous full-color photos. Whether you're a potluck guest or the host, you'll find just the right recipe in this special collection.

To help you locate exactly the type of dish you need, we've organized the recipes in this book into the following handy chapters:

Crowd-Pleasing Specialties. Every potluck guest will love these distinctive dishes, including Roast Beef with Peppers, Mostaccioli Veggie Salad, Parmesan Knots and Chocolate Cream Cake.

Slow Cooker Sensations. Use this potluck-friendly appliance to prepare everything from Slow-Cooked Short Ribs and Hot Ham Sandwiches to No-Fuss Potato Soup and Fruit Salsa.

Fun Finger Foods. For fare with casual flair, take a hands-on approach with Crispy Onion Wings, Super Italian Sub, Caramel Chocolate Cheesecake Bites and Garden Focaccia.

Dishes in a Hurry. Even the busiest cooks will have time to assemble Calico Potato Salad, Southwest Roll-Ups, Tomato Crouton Casserole and Chewy Pecan Pie Bars.

Breakfast Buffets. Start your morning get-togethers off right with Sausage Hash Brown Bake, Cheesy Egg Puffs, No-Knead Citrus Rolls and Strawberry Yogurt Crunch.

One-Dish Wonders. A single bowl, pot, pan or platter is all you'll need to whip up delights like Tangy Pork Barbecue, Maple Baked Beans, Seven-Fruit Salad and Nutty Peach Crisp.

Festive Favorites. On holidays and other special occasions, celebrate with spirited recipes such as Jingle Bell Spread, Jack-o'-Lantern Brownies, Stars and Stripes Torte and Touchdown Cookies.

All the recipes in this book were shared by cooks like you and tested by experienced home economists in the *Taste of Home* Test Kitchen. So you can rest assured that every dish you fix is a tried-and-true success.

Need help finding a particular recipe? Simply flip to the back of the book and glance through the alphabetical index. Or check the general index, which lists recipes by food category, major ingredient and/or cooking method.

In this big cookbook, you'll also see helpful hints to make potlucks easier and more enjoyable. Find tips for keeping foods hot and cold, ways to save time in the kitchen, decorating ideas and much more.

So turn to *Taste of Home's The New Potluck* for every "bring-a-dish" get-together…and make all of your potluck food unforgettable.

"Every potluck guest will love these distinctive dishes…"

crowd-pleasing specialties

Whether your potluck is for a circle of friends or a large group of all ages, you'll have a winning dish when you turn to the recipes in this chapter. They're delightfully different creations, plus tasteful twists on classic favorites—all guaranteed to please a crowd.

Try specialties ranging from cool, creamy Crab-Salad Jumbo Shells (p. 46) to golden Mango Nut Bread (p. 16). No matter which distinctive dishes you choose, you'll want to bring enough for the whole group— because every guest will want to savor a sample.

cream of wild rice soup

J. Beatrice Hintz, Neenah, Wisconsin

Tender chunks of chicken, fresh vegetables and wild rice make this creamy soup a meal in itself. A big steaming bowlful is especially satisfying when the weather's cool, but people enjoy the great flavor year-round.

1 large onion, chopped

1 large carrot, shredded

1 celery rib, chopped

¼ cup butter

½ cup all-purpose flour

8 cups chicken broth

3 cups cooked wild rice

1 cup cubed cooked chicken breast

¼ teaspoon salt

¼ teaspoon pepper

1 cup evaporated milk

¼ cup snipped chives

1 In a large saucepan, saute the onion, carrot and celery in butter until tender. Stir in flour until blended. Gradually add broth. Stir in the rice, chicken, salt and pepper.

2 Bring to a boil over medium heat; cook and stir for 2 minutes or until thickened. Stir in milk; cook 3-5 minutes longer. Garnish with chives.

YIELD: 10 SERVINGS (2½ QUARTS)

banana snack cake

½ cup shortening

¾ cup packed brown sugar

½ cup sugar

2 eggs

1 cup mashed ripe bananas
(2 to 3 medium)

1 teaspoon vanilla extract

2 cups all-purpose *or* whole wheat
flour

1 teaspoon baking soda

1 teaspoon salt

½ cup buttermilk

½ cup chopped nuts

FROSTING:

½ cup packed brown sugar

¼ cup butter

6 tablespoons milk

2½ to 3 cups confectioners' sugar

1 In a mixing bowl, cream shortening and sugars. Add eggs, one at a time, beating well after each addition. Beat in bananas and vanilla. Combine flour, baking soda and salt; add to the creamed mixture alternately with buttermilk. Stir in nuts. Pour into a greased 13-in. x 9-in. x 2-in. baking pan. Bake at 350° for 25-30 minutes or until a toothpick inserted near the center comes out clean. Cool on a wire rack.

2 For frosting, combine brown sugar, butter and milk in a saucepan. Bring to a boil over medium heat; boil and stir for 2 minutes. Remove from the heat; cool to lukewarm. Gradually beat in confectioners' sugar until frosting reaches spreading consistency. Frost the cake.

YIELD: 12 SERVINGS

Dawn Fagerstrom, Warren, Minnesota

Even without the creamy homemade frosting, this moist and nutty cake

is a terrific treat. I often bake it for birthdays and use the recipe to make

cupcakes, too. The yummy banana flavor really comes through.

sour cream cranberry bars

1 cup butter, softened

1 cup packed brown sugar

2 cups quick-cooking oats

1½ cups plus 2 tablespoons all-purpose flour, *divided*

2 cups dried cranberries

1 cup (8 ounces) sour cream

¾ cup sugar

1 egg, lightly beaten

1 tablespoon grated lemon peel

1 teaspoon vanilla extract

1 In a large mixing bowl, cream the butter and brown sugar. Combine the oats and 1½ cups flour; add to the creamed mixture until blended. Set aside 1½ cups for topping. Press remaining crumb mixture into an ungreased 13-in. x 9-in. x 2-in. baking pan. Bake at 350° for 10-12 minutes or until lightly browned.

2 Meanwhile, in a large bowl, combine the cranberries, sour cream, sugar, egg, lemon peel, vanilla and remaining flour. Spread evenly over crust. Sprinkle with reserved crumb mixture. Bake for 20-25 minutes or until lightly browned. Cool on a wire rack. Refrigerate leftovers.

YIELD: ABOUT 3 DOZEN

Barbara Nowakowski, Mesa, Arizona

These sweet-tart bars top a buttery crust with a dried-cranberry filling and golden crumb topping. Easy to prepare, they're a great dessert choice for just about any event, from Christmastime potlucks to summer picnics.

ginger iced tea

Brenda Jeffers, Ottumwa, Iowa

Here's a refreshing beverage that goes well with just about any meal. Carbonated ginger ale makes this tea a wonderful alternative to ordinary iced tea and other soft drinks. Everyone will want a glassful, so be ready to refill the pitcher!

1 cup iced tea mix with lemon and sugar

4 cups water

2 liters ginger ale, chilled

Ice cubes

In a pitcher, combine the iced tea mix and water; refrigerate until chilled. Just before serving, add ginger ale. Serve over ice.

YIELD: 3 QUARTS

impress the host when you're a guest

- When invited to a potluck, ask what kind of dish— whether an appetizer, dessert, salad, etc.—would be best for you to bring.

- Bring your own serving utensils; don't rely on the host to provide exactly what you need.

- Choose recipes that won't require a lot of last-minute preparation at the host's home.

- If you're considering a recipe that would need to be heated in the oven or microwave at the potluck location, ask beforehand if that would be convenient.

- To avoid confusion at cleanup time, label your serving dish with your name...or choose a disposable dish that can simply be thrown away.

sausage sandwich squares

3 to 3½ cups all-purpose flour

1 package (¼ ounce) active dry yeast

½ teaspoon salt

1⅓ cups warm water (120° to 130°)

1 pound bulk Italian sausage

1 sweet red pepper, diced

1 green pepper, diced

1 large onion, diced

4 cups (16 ounces) shredded mozzarella cheese

1 egg

1 tablespoon water

2 tablespoons grated Parmesan cheese

2 tablespoons minced fresh parsley

½ teaspoon dried oregano

⅛ teaspoon garlic powder

1 In a bowl, combine 2 cups flour, yeast and salt. Add warm water; mix well. Add enough remaining flour to form a firm dough. Turn onto a floured surface; knead until smooth and elastic, about 6 minutes. Place in a greased bowl, turning once to grease top. Cover and let rise in a warm place until doubled, about 50 minutes.

2 In a skillet, cook sausage until no longer pink; remove with a slotted spoon and set aside. In the drippings, saute peppers and onion until tender; drain. Press half of the dough onto the bottom and ½ in. up the sides of a greased 15-in. x 10-in. x 1-in. baking pan. Spread sausage evenly over the crust. Top with peppers and onion. Sprinkle with mozzarella cheese.

3 Roll out remaining dough to fit pan; place over cheese and seal the edges. In a small bowl, beat egg and water. Add remaining ingredients; mix well. Brush over dough. Cut slits in top. Bake at 400° for 20-25 minutes or until golden brown. Cut into squares.

YIELD: 12-15 SERVINGS

Mary Merrill, Bloomingdale, Ohio
I came up with this recipe when I needed to feed a bunch of hungry teenagers. Since then, I've found that the warm squares appeal to everyone. The pizza-like sandwich features Italian sausage and mozzarella.

parmesan knots

½ cup vegetable oil

¼ cup grated Parmesan cheese

1½ teaspoons dried parsley flakes

1½ teaspoons dried oregano

1 teaspoon garlic powder

Dash pepper

3 cans (12 ounces *each*) refrigerated buttermilk biscuits

1 In a small bowl, combine oil, cheese, parsley, oregano, garlic powder and pepper; set aside. Cut each biscuit in half. Roll each portion into a 6-in. rope; tie in a loose knot. Place on greased baking sheets.

2 Bake at 450° for 6-8 minutes or until golden brown. Immediately brush with the Parmesan mixture, then brush again. Serve warm.

YIELD: 5 DOZEN

Cathy Adams, Parkersburg, West Virginia

I use refrigerated buttermilk biscuit dough to make these buttery rolls.

Everyone comments on the Parmesan cheese and flavorful mix of seasonings.

mango nut bread

Jo Sherley, Kahului, Hawaii

We live on the slopes of Haleakala, where carrots, potatoes, cabbage, bananas, litchis and mangoes are grown. This is my favorite recipe using mangoes. Spiced with cinnamon, the moist loaves never last very long.

2 cups all-purpose flour

1½ cups sugar

1 teaspoon baking soda

½ teaspoon salt

½ teaspoon ground cinnamon

3 eggs

½ cup vegetable oil

1 teaspoon vanilla extract

2 cups chopped mangoes

½ cup chopped dates

½ cup chopped walnuts *or* macadamia nuts

1 In a large bowl, combine the first five ingredients. In another bowl, beat eggs, oil and vanilla. Stir into dry ingredients just until moistened. Fold in mangoes, dates and nuts (batter will be stiff). Spoon into two greased 8-in. x 4-in. x 2-in. loaf pans.

2 Bake at 350° for 50-55 minutes or until a toothpick inserted near the center comes out clean. Cool for 10 minutes before removing from pans to wire racks.

YIELD: 2 LOAVES

mexican lasagna

2 pounds ground beef

1 can (16 ounces) refried beans

1 can (4 ounces) chopped green chilies

1 envelope taco seasoning

2 tablespoons hot salsa

12 ounces uncooked lasagna noodles

4 cups (16 ounces) shredded Co-Jack or Monterey Jack cheese, *divided*

1 jar (16 ounces) mild salsa

2 cups water

2 cups (16 ounces) sour cream

1 can (2¼ ounces) sliced ripe olives, drained

3 green onions, chopped

1 In a skillet, cook beef over medium heat until no longer pink; drain. Add the beans, chilies, taco seasoning and hot salsa; mix well. In a greased 13-in. x 9-in. x 2-in. baking dish, layer a third of the noodles and meat mixture. Sprinkle with 1 cup of cheese. Repeat layers twice. Combine mild salsa and water; pour over top.

2 Cover and bake at 350° for 1 hour or until heated through. Uncover; top with sour cream, olives, onions and remaining cheese. Bake 5 minutes longer. Let stand 10-15 minutes before cutting.

YIELD: 12 SERVINGS

Rose Ann Buhle, Minooka, Illinois

I collect recipes, and my husband jokes that I'll never be able to prepare them all. But I'm glad I tried this deliciously different lasagna. The combination of popular Mexican ingredients and pasta is always a crowd favorite.

all-occasion punch

2 quarts cold water

3 cans (6 ounces *each*) frozen lemonade, thawed

2 quarts ginger ale, chilled

1 quart Cherry 7-Up, chilled

Ice ring, optional

In a punch bowl, combine water and lemonade. Stir in ginger ale and 7-Up. Top with an ice ring if desired. Serve immediately.

YIELD: 5½ QUARTS

Carol Van Sickle, Versailles, Kentucky

People are surprised when they discover how simple this refreshing, thirst-quenching beverage is. The pretty pink color is especially nice for baby or bridal showers, but the punch disappears no matter where I serve it.

four-cheese bow ties

Mary Farney, Normal, Illinois

My daughter-in-law shared this family-favorite recipe with me, and now it's popular in our family, too. An abundance of cheese makes this meatless dish rich and filling. With tomatoes and parsley, it's also beautiful on a buffet table.

2 cans (14$\frac{1}{2}$ ounces *each*) diced tomatoes

1 package (16 ounces) bow tie pasta

$\frac{1}{4}$ cup butter

$\frac{1}{4}$ cup all-purpose flour

$\frac{1}{4}$ teaspoon salt

$\frac{1}{4}$ teaspoon pepper

1$\frac{1}{2}$ cups milk

1$\frac{1}{2}$ cups (6 ounces) shredded mozzarella cheese

1$\frac{1}{3}$ cups grated Romano cheese

$\frac{1}{2}$ cup shredded Parmesan cheese

$\frac{1}{4}$ cup crumbled blue *or* Gorgonzola cheese

$\frac{1}{2}$ cup minced fresh parsley

1 Drain tomatoes, reserving 1$\frac{1}{4}$ cups juice; set aside. Cook pasta according to package directions; drain.

2 In a saucepan, melt butter over medium heat. Stir in the flour, salt and pepper until smooth; gradually add milk and reserved tomato juice. Bring to a boil; cook and stir for 2 minutes or until thickened. Remove from the heat.

3 In a large bowl, combine the pasta, sauce and reserved tomatoes. Stir in the cheeses and parsley; toss gently. Place in a greased 3$\frac{1}{2}$-qt. baking dish. Bake, uncovered, at 375° for 30-35 minutes or until golden and bubbly.

YIELD: 12 SERVINGS

special shrimp bake

3 quarts water

1 tablespoon plus 1 teaspoon salt, *divided*

2½ pounds uncooked medium shrimp, peeled and deveined

2 tablespoons vegetable oil

1 tablespoon lemon juice

¼ cup finely chopped green pepper

¼ cup finely chopped onion

2 tablespoons butter

1 can (10¾ ounces) condensed tomato soup, undiluted

1 cup heavy whipping cream

2¼ cups cooked rice

⅛ teaspoon *each* ground mace, pepper and cayenne pepper

½ cup slivered almonds, toasted, *divided*

1 In a Dutch oven, bring water and 1 tablespoon salt to a boil. Add shrimp; cook for 3 minutes or until pink. Drain. Sprinkle shrimp with oil and lemon juice; set aside.

2 In a skillet, saute green pepper and onion in butter for 5 minutes or until tender. Add soup, cream, rice, mace, pepper, cayenne, ¼ cup of almonds and remaining salt. Set aside 1 cup of shrimp. Add remaining shrimp to the rice mixture. Transfer to a greased 2-qt. baking dish.

3 Bake, uncovered, at 350° for 30-35 minutes. Top with reserved shrimp and remaining almonds; bake 20 minutes longer or until the shrimp are lightly browned.

YIELD: 8-10 SERVINGS

Kathy Houchen, Waldorf, Maryland

With rice and vegetables, this delicious shrimp dish is a satisfying meal-in-one. The recipe offers make-ahead convenience, too. If I need to, I can assemble the casserole the night before, refrigerate it and pop it in the oven the next day.

roast beef with peppers

3 tablespoons vegetable oil

1 boneless beef rump roast
(3 pounds)

3 cups hot water

4 teaspoons beef bouillon granules

1 tablespoon dried oregano

1 to 2 garlic cloves, minced

½ teaspoon salt

½ teaspoon pepper

3 medium bell peppers, julienned

3 tablespoons butter

1 In a Dutch oven, heat oil over medium-high heat. Brown roast on all sides; drain. Combine the water, bouillon, oregano, garlic, salt and pepper; pour over roast.

2 Cover and bake at 350° for 3 hours or until meat is tender. Remove roast to a warm serving platter. Let stand 10 minutes before slicing. Meanwhile, in a skillet, saute peppers in butter until tender. Serve peppers and pan juices with the roast.

YIELD: 8-10 SERVINGS

Jeanne Murray, Scottsbluff, Nebraska

This moist, flavorful roast gets a bit of Italian flair from oregano and garlic. The sauteed peppers not only are a fresh-tasting accompaniment to the meat, they look beautiful arranged around the sliced roast on a platter.

cordon bleu casserole

Joyce Paul, Moose Jaw, Saskatchewan

When I'm invited to a potluck, people usually ask me to bring this tempting casserole. Chunks of turkey and ham are wonderful in the creamy sauce. To finish it off, I sprinkle on a cheesy bread-crumb topping.

4 cups cubed cooked turkey

3 cups cubed fully cooked ham

1 cup (4 ounces) shredded cheddar cheese

1 cup chopped onion

1/4 cup butter

1/3 cup all-purpose flour

2 cups half-and-half cream

1 teaspoon dill weed

1/8 teaspoon ground mustard

1/8 teaspoon ground nutmeg

TOPPING:

1 cup dry bread crumbs

2 tablespoons butter, melted

1/4 teaspoon dill weed

1/4 cup shredded cheddar cheese

1/4 cup chopped walnuts

1 In a large bowl, combine turkey, ham and cheese; set aside. In a saucepan, saute onion in butter until tender. Add flour; stir to form a paste. Gradually add cream, stirring constantly. Bring to a boil; boil 1 minute or until thick. Add dill, mustard and nutmeg; mix well. Remove from the heat and pour over meat mixture.

2 Spoon into a greased 13-in. x 9-in. x 2-in. baking dish. Toss bread crumbs, butter and dill; stir in cheese and walnuts. Sprinkle over the casserole. Bake, uncovered, at 350° for 30 minutes or until heated through.

YIELD: 8-10 SERVINGS

set a special tone for your potluck

Want to add extra fun to a potluck you're hosting? Consider giving it a theme. Request that guests bring a food that fits the "flavor" of the meal.

Remember to choose a theme that isn't too limiting—you don't want to make it difficult for guests to find an appropriate recipe. Examples of themes that offer plenty of recipe options are Tex-Mex, Hawaiian/tropical and Italian.

To make your event especially memorable, accent your home with coordinating decorations. Enhance the meal with mood-setting music.

beans 'n' greens

1 cup olive oil

¼ cup cider vinegar

1½ teaspoons salt

1½ teaspoons sugar

½ teaspoon celery seed

½ teaspoon paprika

2 cans (14½ ounces *each*) cut green beans, drained *or* 4 cups cooked cut fresh green beans (2-inch pieces)

8 cups torn lettuce

4 cups torn fresh spinach

2 cups (8 ounces) shredded Swiss cheese

In a jar with a tight-fitting lid, combine the first six ingredients; shake well. Pour over green beans; let stand for 15 minutes. Just before serving, drain beans, reserving the marinade. In a salad bowl, combine the beans, lettuce, spinach and Swiss cheese. Drizzle with the reserved marinade and toss to coat.

YIELD: 14-18 SERVINGS

Dorothy Pritchett, Wills Point, Texas

Don't let the simple name fool you—this salad is special enough to star on a buffet table. A homemade vinegar-oil marinade gives the green beans, lettuce and spinach great flavor, and shredded Swiss cheese adds extra appeal.

chicken asparagus pasta supper

4 tablespoons vegetable oil, *divided*

1½ pounds fresh asparagus, cut into 2-inch pieces

8 ounces sliced fresh mushrooms

1½ cups fresh broccoli florets

2 medium carrots, cut into julienne strips

2 medium zucchini, sliced

3 green onions, sliced into ½-inch pieces

½ teaspoon salt

4 boneless skinless chicken breasts, cut into 1-inch pieces

½ cup frozen peas

SAUCE:

2 tablespoons butter

2 tablespoons all-purpose flour

1 teaspoon chicken bouillon granules

2 cups milk

¼ teaspoon pepper

1 pound thin spaghetti, cooked and drained

1 Heat 2 tablespoons oil in a large skillet over medium-high heat. Add the asparagus, mushrooms, broccoli, carrots, zucchini, onions and salt. Cook and stir for 5 minutes. Remove vegetables from skillet; set aside. Add remaining oil to skillet. Cook and stir chicken for 5-6 minutes or until no longer pink, stirring constantly. Return vegetables to skillet; add peas and cook for 3-5 minutes. Set aside.

2 For sauce, melt butter in a medium saucepan over low heat. Stir in flour to form a smooth paste. Add bouillon. Gradually add milk, stirring constantly until sauce is thickened. Season with pepper. Pour over chicken/vegetable mixture; toss to coat. Serve over spaghetti.

YIELD: 8 SERVINGS

Ginny Truwe, Mankato, Minnesota

My family can't get enough of this delicious all-in-one dinner. Coated with a creamy white sauce, the tender chicken and vegetables are served over spaghetti. I love bringing this dish to potlucks because it's a hit every time.

crab-salad jumbo shells

30 jumbo pasta shells

1 cup finely chopped fresh broccoli florets

1 garlic clove, minced

2 packages (8 ounces *each*) imitation crabmeat, chopped

1 cup (8 ounces) sour cream

½ cup mayonnaise

¼ cup finely shredded carrot

¼ cup diced seeded peeled cucumber

1 tablespoon chopped green onion

1 teaspoon dill weed

Cook pasta according to package directions; rinse in cold water and drain well. In a microwave-safe bowl, combine the broccoli and garlic. Cover and microwave on high for 1 minute or until crisp-tender. Transfer to a large bowl; stir in the remaining ingredients. Stuff into pasta shells. Cover and refrigerate overnight.

YIELD: 30 STUFFED SHELLS

JoAnne Anderson, Knoxville, Iowa

I received this recipe from a friend and adjusted the ingredients to suit my family's tastes. It's a fun and flavorful way to serve crab salad.

sparkling rhubarb salad

4 cups diced fresh *or* frozen rhubarb

1½ cups water

½ cup sugar

1 package (6 ounces) strawberry-flavored gelatin

1 cup fresh orange juice

1 tablespoon grated orange peel

2 cups sliced fresh strawberries

In a saucepan, combine rhubarb, water and sugar. Cook over medium heat until the rhubarb is tender, 5-10 minutes. Remove from the heat. Stir in gelatin until dissolved. Add orange juice and peel. Chill until slightly thickened, 2 to 2½ hours. Add strawberries; pour into a 2-qt. bowl. Chill until firm, about 2-3 hours.

YIELD: 8-10 SERVINGS

Mary Ellen Beachy, Dundee, Ohio

My rhubarb patch usually produces a lot, and this recipe is a wonderful way to use up my bountiful summer harvest. Strawberries lend sweet, fresh flavor to the jewel-red gelatin, which looks beautiful on a buffet table.

lemon ladyfinger dessert

Katherine Buch, Waterford, New Jersey

This impressive dessert appears complicated and time-consuming to make, but it actually comes together quickly using purchased ladyfingers. The tangy lemon flavor, cream filling and soft cookies are a heavenly combination.

1 package (3 ounces) lemon gelatin

1 cup confectioners' sugar

2 cups boiling water

2 cups heavy whipping cream

1/2 teaspoon almond extract

1 teaspoon grated lemon peel

1 package (3 ounces) ladyfingers

Lemon peel strips, optional

1 In a mixing bowl, dissolve gelatin and sugar in water; stir until completely dissolved. Refrigerate until syrupy, about 45 minutes. Add cream and extract; beat until cream mixture mounds slightly, about 10 minutes. Fold in lemon peel.

2 Split ladyfingers and arrange upright around the edge of a 2 1/2-qt. serving bowl (about 8-in. diameter). Set aside any unused ladyfingers for garnish or another use. Pour cream mixture into bowl. Garnish with remaining ladyfingers and lemon peel strips if desired. Cover and refrigerate for 2-3 hours.

YIELD: 8-10 SERVINGS

potatoes supreme

8 to 10 medium potatoes, peeled and cubed

1 can (10¾ ounces) condensed cream of chicken soup, undiluted

3 cups (12 ounces) shredded cheddar cheese, *divided*

1 cup (8 ounces) sour cream

3 green onions, chopped

Salt and pepper to taste

1 Place potatoes in a saucepan and cover with water. Bring to a boil; cover and cook until almost tender. Drain and cool. Combine soup, 1½ cups cheese, sour cream, onions, salt and pepper; stir in potatoes.

2 Place in a greased 13-in. x 9-in x 2-in. baking dish. Sprinkle with remaining cheese. Bake, uncovered, at 350° for 25-30 minutes or until heated through.

YIELD: 8-10 SERVINGS

Mrs. Afton Johnson, Sugar City, Idaho
Potato-lovers can't seem to get enough of this cheesy and creamy side dish, which is a family favorite. It's simple to assemble, too. The recipe requires only cubed potatoes, salt, pepper and four other ingredients.

blueberry lattice bars

1 cup butter, softened

½ cup sugar

1 egg

2¾ cups all-purpose flour

½ teaspoon vanilla extract

¼ teaspoon salt

FILLING:

3 cups fresh *or* frozen blueberries

1 cup sugar

3 tablespoons cornstarch

1 In a mixing bowl, cream butter and sugar. Add the egg, flour, vanilla and salt; mix well. Cover and refrigerate for 2 hours. Meanwhile, in a saucepan, bring the blueberries, sugar and cornstarch to a boil. Cook and stir for 2 minutes or until thickened.

2 Roll two-thirds of the dough into a 14-in. x 10-in. rectangle. Place in a greased 13-in. x 9-in. x 2-in. baking dish. Top with filling. Roll out remaining dough to ¼ -in. thickness. Cut into ½ -in.-wide strips; make a lattice crust over filling. Bake at 375° for 30-35 minutes or until top is golden brown. Cool on a wire rack. Cut into bars.

YIELD: 2 DOZEN

Debbie Ayers, Baileyville, Maine

Our area has an annual blueberry festival, and my daughters and I are constantly looking for great new berry recipes to enter in the cooking contest. When we submitted these wonderful pie-like bars, they received a blue ribbon.

slow cooker sensations

54

73

Cook…transport…serve…it's all possible with a slow cooker. Plug it in on the buffet table, and it'll keep food hot, too. That's why this common kitchen appliance is a favorite of people who frequent potlucks.

Choose family-pleasing Chili Mac (p. 54), flavorful Hot Ham Sandwiches (p. 73) or any of the other delicious slow-cooked main dishes, side dishes, soups and appetizers included in this chapter. Not only are these recipes easy to assemble in advance, they're sure to stand out among the potluck crowd.

chili mac

Marie Posavec, Berwyn, Illinois

This hearty beef-and-pasta dish is not only a real crowd-pleaser at potlucks and parties, but it's also a regular on my family dinner menu. Sometimes I turn this recipe into a satisfying soup by adding a can of beef broth.

1 pound ground beef, cooked and drained

2 cans (15 ounces *each*) hot chili beans, undrained

2 large green peppers, chopped

1 large onion, chopped

4 celery ribs, chopped

1 can (8 ounces) tomato sauce

1 envelope chili seasoning

2 garlic cloves, minced

1 package (7 ounces) elbow macaroni, cooked and drained

Salt and pepper to taste

In a slow cooker, combine the first eight ingredients; mix well. Cover and cook on low for 6 hours or until heated through. Stir in macaroni; mix well. Season with salt and pepper.

YIELD: 12 SERVINGS

reuben spread

1 jar (16 ounces) sauerkraut, rinsed and drained

1 package (8 ounces) cream cheese, cubed

2 cups (8 ounces) shredded Swiss cheese

1 package (3 ounces) deli corned beef, chopped

3 tablespoons Thousand Island salad dressing

Snack rye bread *or* crackers

In a 1½-qt. slow cooker, combine the first five ingredients. Cover and cook for 2 hours or until cheeses are melted; stir to blend. Serve warm with bread or crackers.

YIELD: 3½ CUPS

Rosalie Fuchs, Paynesville, Minnesota

I received this easy five-ingredient recipe from my daughter. Everyone says it's like eating a traditional reuben sandwich as a spread. To keep it warm while serving, just leave it in the slow cooker on low.

slow-cooked short ribs

2/3 cup all-purpose flour

2 teaspoons salt

1/2 teaspoon pepper

4 to 4 1/2 pounds boneless beef short ribs

1/4 to 1/3 cup butter

1 large onion, chopped

1 1/2 cups beef broth

3/4 cup red wine vinegar

3/4 cup packed brown sugar

1/2 cup chili sauce

1/3 cup ketchup

1/3 cup Worcestershire sauce

5 garlic cloves, minced

1 1/2 teaspoons chili powder

1 In a large resealable plastic bag, combine the flour, salt and pepper. Add ribs in batches and shake to coat. In a large skillet, brown ribs in butter. Transfer to a 5-qt. slow cooker.

2 In the same skillet, combine the remaining ingredients. Cook and stir until mixture comes to a boil; pour over ribs (slow cooker will be full). Cover and cook on low for 9-10 hours or until meat is tender.

YIELD: 12-15 SERVINGS

Pam Halfhill, Medina, Ohio

Smothered in a mouth-watering barbecue sauce, these meaty ribs are a popular entree wherever I serve them. The recipe is great for time-crunched cooks—after the ingredients are combined, the slow cooker does all the work.

italian turkey sandwiches

Carol Riley, Galva, Illinois

My family loves these flavorful turkey sandwiches. The recipe makes a lot, so it's also a great choice when I need a main dish to bring to a potluck or party. If I have any leftovers, they taste just as good reheated for lunch or dinner the next day.

1 bone-in turkey breast (5½ pounds), skin removed

½ cup chopped green pepper

1 medium onion, chopped

¼ cup chili sauce

3 tablespoons white vinegar

2 tablespoons dried oregano *or* Italian seasoning

4 teaspoons beef bouillon granules

11 kaiser *or* hard sandwich rolls, split

1 Place the turkey breast, green pepper and onion in a 5-qt. slow cooker coated with nonstick cooking spray. Combine the chili sauce, vinegar, oregano and bouillon; pour over turkey and vegetables. Cover and cook on low for 5-6 hours or until meat juices run clear and vegetables are tender.

2 Remove turkey with a slotted spoon, reserving cooking liquid. Shred the turkey with two forks; return to cooking juices. Spoon ½ cup onto each roll.

YIELD: 11 SERVINGS

cranberry apple cider

4 cups water

4 cups apple juice

1 can (12 ounces) frozen apple juice concentrate, thawed

1 medium apple, peeled and sliced

1 cup fresh *or* frozen cranberries

1 medium orange, peeled and sectioned

1 cinnamon stick

In a slow cooker, combine all ingredients; mix well. Cover and cook on low for 2 hours or until cider reaches desired temperature. Discard cinnamon stick. If desired, remove fruit with a slotted spoon before serving.

YIELD: 10 SERVINGS (ABOUT 2½ QUARTS)

Jennifer Naboka, North Plainfield, New Jersey

Served warm from the slow cooker, this soothing beverage proves especially popular when the weather's cool. Cranberries and orange sections add a tangy twist to the spiced cider. It's ideal for gatherings during the Christmas season, and my husband also likes to take it with him on hunting trips.

hot bacon cheese dip

2 packages (8 ounces *each*) cream cheese, cubed

4 cups (16 ounces) shredded cheddar cheese

1 cup half-and-half cream

2 teaspoons Worcestershire sauce

1 teaspoon dried minced onion

1 teaspoon prepared mustard

16 bacon strips, cooked and crumbled

Tortilla chips *or* French bread slices

In a 1½-qt. slow cooker, combine the first six ingredients. Cover and cook for 2 hours or until cheeses are melted, stirring occasionally. Just before serving, stir in bacon. Serve warm with tortilla chips or bread.

YIELD: 4 CUPS

Susan Whitaker, Knoxville, Tennessee

I've tried a variety of appetizers before, but this one is a sure people-pleaser. The thick dip has lots of bacon flavor and keeps everyone happily munching. I serve it with tortilla chips or sliced French bread.

pork chili

2½ pounds boneless pork, cut into 1-inch cubes

2 tablespoons vegetable oil

1 can (28 ounces) diced tomatoes, undrained

1 can (15½ ounces) chili beans, undrained

1 can (8 ounces) tomato sauce

¼ cup salsa

¼ cup chopped onion

¼ cup chopped green pepper

1 tablespoon chili powder

1 teaspoon minced jalapeno pepper

¼ teaspoon garlic powder

¼ teaspoon cayenne powder

¼ teaspoon pepper

¼ teaspoon salt

In a large skillet over medium-high heat, brown pork in oil; drain. Place in a slow cooker; add remaining ingredients. Cover and cook on high for 2 hours. Reduce heat to low and cook 4 hours longer.

YIELD: 10-12 SERVINGS

EDITOR'S NOTE: When cutting or seeding hot peppers, use rubber or plastic gloves to protect your hands. Avoid touching your face.

Linda Temple, St. Joseph, Missouri
My husband usually tries to avoid spending time in the kitchen, but he'll frequently offer to prepare a batch of this delicious chili. Of course, he always eagerly serves as taste-tester!

tangy beef and vegetable stew

6 cups cubed peeled potatoes
(1/2-inch pieces)

8 medium carrots, cut into
1/2-inch pieces

2 medium onions, cubed

4 pounds lean beef stew meat,
cut into 1-inch pieces

1/3 cup vegetable oil

1/3 cup all-purpose flour

4 beef bouillon cubes

3 cups boiling water

1/3 cup vinegar

1/3 cup ketchup

3 tablespoons prepared horseradish

3 tablespoons prepared mustard

2 tablespoons sugar

2 cups *each* frozen peas and corn

2 cups sliced fresh mushrooms

1 Place the potatoes, carrots and onions in a large slow cooker. In a large skillet, brown beef in oil, a single layer at a time; place over the vegetables. Sprinkle with flour.

2 Dissolve bouillon cubes in boiling water. Stir in vinegar, ketchup, horseradish, mustard and sugar; pour over meat and vegetables. Cover and cook on high for 5 hours. Add peas, corn and mushrooms. Cover and cook on high for 45 minutes.

YIELD: 12-16 SERVINGS

EDITOR'S NOTE: Cooking times may vary with slow cookers.

Amberleah Holmberg, Calgary, Alberta

This hearty meal-in-one is sure to satisfy even the biggest appetites at your get-together. I combine chunks of beef stew meat with potatoes, carrots and plenty of other veggies. Mustard and horseradish add to the great flavor.

fun finger foods

104

86

Make it casual…make it relaxed…make it fun with no-utensils-required recipes. You'll be surprised at the wide range of sensational options in this hands-on chapter, including fresh Garden Focaccia (pg. 104) and Apple Cinnamon Turnovers (p. 86).

These fantastic finger foods add to the easygoing atmosphere at friendly get-togethers, and they're just as delicious and satisfying as any fork-and-knife fare. So go ahead—set aside the silverware. You'll have popular potluck food well in hand.

almond tea cakes

Janet Fennema Ringelberg, Troy, Ontario

I have a hectic schedule, but when I can find a few spare moments, I love to bake. These elegant filled cakes topped with sliced almonds are a favorite of mine. I usually double the recipe and freeze half for later.

2 cups butter

¾ cup sugar

¾ cup packed brown sugar

2 eggs

4 teaspoons almond extract

4 cups all-purpose flour

1 teaspoon baking powder

FILLING:

1 egg white

½ cup sugar

½ cup ground almonds

½ teaspoon lemon juice

Milk

Sliced almonds

1 In a mixing bowl, cream butter and sugars. Add eggs and extract; mix well. Add flour and baking powder (dough will be soft). Chill.

2 For filling, stir egg white, sugar, almonds and lemon juice in a small bowl. Remove a portion of the dough at a time from the refrigerator. Place 1-in. balls of dough into miniature muffin cups, pressing slightly into sides and bottom. Place ½ teaspoon of filling into each.

3 Cover with quarter-sized circles of dough. Brush with a little milk and top with an almond. Bake at 350° for 20-25 minutes or until golden.

YIELD: ABOUT 5 DOZEN

apple cinnamon turnovers

1 medium tart apple, peeled and chopped

½ cup applesauce

¾ teaspoon ground cinnamon, *divided*

Dash ground nutmeg

1 tube (7½ ounces) refrigerated biscuits

1 tablespoon butter, melted

2 tablespoons sugar

1 In a bowl, combine the apple, applesauce, ¼ teaspoon cinnamon and nutmeg. Separate biscuits; roll out each into a 6-in. circle. Place on greased baking sheets. Place a heaping tablespoonful of apple mixture in the center of each. Fold in half and pinch edges to seal.

2 Brush turnovers with butter. Combine sugar and remaining cinnamon; sprinkle over tops. Bake at 400° for 8-10 minutes or until edges are golden brown. Serve warm.

YIELD: 10 SERVINGS

Robin Stevens, Cadiz, Kentucky

Refrigerated biscuits speed up the preparation of these wonderful dessert-or-breakfast turnovers. Sprinkled with cinnamon and sugar, they get rave reviews at potlucks. People say the taste reminds them of apple pie.

spinach phyllo bundles

1 medium onion, chopped

2 tablespoons plus ½ cup butter, *divided*

1 package (10 ounces) frozen chopped spinach, thawed and squeezed dry

1 cup (4 ounces) crumbled feta cheese

¾ cup small-curd cottage cheese

3 eggs, lightly beaten

¼ cup dry bread crumbs

¾ teaspoon salt

½ teaspoon dill weed

Pepper to taste

1 package (16 ounces) frozen phyllo dough, thawed

1 In a large skillet, saute onion in 2 tablespoons butter until tender. Remove from the heat. Stir in the spinach, feta cheese, cottage cheese, eggs, bread crumbs, salt, dill and pepper.

2 Use one package of phyllo sheets. (Save the remaining phyllo for another use.) Melt remaining butter. Layer and brush five phyllo sheets with melted butter. Keep remaining phyllo covered to avoid drying out.

3 Cut buttered sheets lengthwise into 2-in. strips; cut in half widthwise. Place 1 heaping tablespoon of filling at one end of each strip; fold into a triangle, as you would fold a flag. Place on an ungreased baking sheet. Brush with butter. Bake at 400° for 15-20 minutes or until golden brown. Serve warm.

YIELD: 28 APPETIZERS

EDITOR'S NOTE: This recipe was tested with Athenos phyllo dough. The phyllo sheets measure 18 in. x 14 in.

Eloise Olive, Greensboro, North Carolina

These cheesy triangles were inspired by spanakopita, a Greek pie made with phyllo dough. Working with that dough requires a little extra care to prevent it from drying out, but these delicious bundles are well worth the effort.

fruit kabobs

Cheryl Ollis, Matthews, North Carolina

To perk up a plain platter of fresh fruit, just rely on this easy recipe. It combines pineapple chunks, grapes, strawberries and more on wooden skewers and accents them with a yummy orange-coconut dip.

- 1 medium tart apple, cut into 1-inch chunks
- 1 medium pear, cut into 1-inch chunks
- 1 tablespoon lemon juice
- 1 can (8 ounces) pineapple chunks, drained
- 24 grapes (about ¼ pound)
- 24 fresh strawberries

COCONUT DIP:
- 1½ cups vanilla yogurt
- 4½ teaspoons flaked coconut
- 4½ teaspoons orange marmalade

Toss apple and pear with lemon juice. Divide fruit into 12 portions and thread onto wooden skewers. Combine dip ingredients in a small bowl; serve with the kabobs.

YIELD: 12 KABOBS

keep fresh fruit at its best

When you plan to serve fresh fruit on a platter or in a salad, keep in mind that fruits such as strawberries, cantaloupe and pineapple may be cut a day in advance of your meal. Store each variety of fruit in a separate container in the refrigerator.

Fruits such as apples and bananas are best when cut just before serving. Tossing fresh-cut pieces of those fruits in lemon or orange juice helps prevent browning.

lime cooler bars

2 1/2 cups all-purpose flour, *divided*

1/2 cup confectioners' sugar

3/4 cup cold butter

4 eggs

2 cups sugar

1/3 cup lime juice

1/2 teaspoon lime peel

1/2 teaspoon baking powder

Additional confectioners' sugar

1 In a bowl, combine 2 cups flour and confectioners' sugar; cut in butter until mixture resembles coarse crumbs. Pat into a greased 13-in. x 9-in. x 2-in. baking pan. Bake at 350° for 20 minutes or until lightly browned.

2 In a bowl, whisk the eggs, sugar, lime juice and peel until frothy. Combine the baking powder and remaining flour; whisk in egg mixture. Pour over hot crust. Bake for 20-25 minutes or until light golden brown. Cool on a wire rack. Dust with confectioners' sugar. Cut into squares.

YIELD: 3 DOZEN

Dorothy Anderson, Ottawa, Kansas

With a tangy "twist" of lime juice, these tempting bars offer a burst of citrus flavor in every bite. I often rely on this recipe because it's an easy-to-make dessert that tastes special. If you like, garnish each bar with cut fresh lime.

spice cupcakes

2 cups water

1 cup raisins

½ cup shortening

1 cup sugar

1 egg

1¾ cups all-purpose flour

1 teaspoon baking soda

½ teaspoon salt

½ teaspoon *each* ground allspice, cloves, cinnamon and nutmeg

¼ cup chopped walnuts

FROSTING:

1 cup packed brown sugar

⅓ cup half-and-half cream

¼ teaspoon salt

3 tablespoons butter

1 teaspoon vanilla extract

1¼ cups confectioners' sugar

Coarsely chopped walnuts, optional

1 In a saucepan, bring water and raisins to a boil. Reduce heat; simmer for 10 minutes. Remove from heat and set aside (do not drain). In a mixing bowl, cream shortening and sugar. Add egg and raisins.

2 Combine dry ingredients; add to creamed mixture and mix well. Stir in walnuts. Fill greased or paper-lined muffin cups with ⅓ cup batter each. Bake at 350° for 20-25 minutes or until a toothpick comes out clean. Cool for 10 minutes; remove from pan to a wire rack.

3 For frosting, combine brown sugar, cream and salt in a saucepan. Bring to a boil over medium-low heat; cook and stir until smooth. Stir in butter and vanilla. Remove from heat; cool slightly. Stir in confectioners' sugar until smooth. Frost cupcakes; top with nuts if desired.

YIELD: 14 CUPCAKES

Carla Hodenfield, New Town, North Dakota

These moist spicy cupcakes with creamy caramel frosting and walnuts are a delicious treat. They have all the goodness of a made-from-scratch dessert but don't take a long time to prepare, so I'm always happy to whip up a batch.

coconut pecan cookies

Diane Selich, Vassar, Michigan

With chocolate chips and coconut in the batter and a yummy pecan-coconut frosting, these golden brown cookies will remind you of German chocolate cake. A drizzle of chocolate tops them off in a festive way.

1 egg, lightly beaten

1 can (5 ounces) evaporated milk

2/3 cup sugar

1/4 cup butter, cubed

1 1/3 cups flaked coconut

1/2 cup chopped pecans

COOKIE DOUGH:

1 cup butter, softened

3/4 cup sugar

3/4 cup packed brown sugar

2 eggs

1 teaspoon vanilla extract

2 1/4 cups all-purpose flour

1 teaspoon baking soda

1 teaspoon salt

4 cups (24 ounces) semisweet chocolate chips, *divided*

1/4 cup flaked coconut

1 For frosting, in a saucepan, combine the egg, milk, sugar and butter. Cook and stir over medium-low heat for 10-12 minutes or until slightly thickened and mixture reaches 160°. Stir in coconut and pecans. Set aside.

2 In a mixing bowl, cream butter and sugars. Add eggs, one at a time, beating well after each addition. Beat in vanilla. Combine the flour, baking soda and salt; gradually add to creamed mixture. Stir in 2 cups chips and coconut.

3 Drop by tablespoonfuls 2 in. apart onto ungreased baking sheets. Bake at 350° for 8-10 minutes or until lightly browned. Cool for 10 minutes before removing to wire racks to cool completely.

4 In a microwave, melt the remaining chocolate chips; stir until smooth. Frost cooled cookies, then drizzle with melted chocolate.

YIELD: 6 1/2 DOZEN

crispy onion wings

12 whole chicken wings (about 2½ pounds)

2½ cups crushed potato chips

1 can (2.8 ounces) french-fried onions, crushed

½ cup cornmeal

2 teaspoons dried oregano

1 teaspoon onion salt

1 teaspoon garlic powder

1 teaspoon paprika

2 eggs, beaten

¼ cup butter, melted

1 Line a 15-in. x 10-in. x 1-in. baking pan with foil and grease the foil; set aside. Cut chicken wings into three sections; discard wing tip section. In a large resealable plastic bag, combine the potato chips, onions, cornmeal and seasonings; mix well. Dip the chicken wings in eggs. Place in the bag, a few at a time; shake to coat and press crumb mixture into chicken.

2 Place wings in prepared pan; drizzle with butter. Bake, uncovered, at 375° for 30-35 minutes or until chicken juices run clear and coating is crisp.

YIELD: 2 DOZEN

EDITOR'S NOTE: 2½ pounds of uncooked chicken wing sections (wingettes) may be substituted for the whole chicken wings. Omit cutting wings and discarding tips.

Jonathan Hershey, Akron, Ohio

My family and I often enjoy these buttery wings on weekends. The crisp coating of french-fried onions, potato chips and cornmeal is also great on the chicken tenders I make from cut-up chicken breasts.

sweet-sour deviled eggs

12 hard-cooked eggs

1/3 cup plus 1 tablespoon mayonnaise

5 teaspoons sugar

5 teaspoons cider vinegar

1 teaspoon prepared mustard

1/2 teaspoon salt

1/4 teaspoon pepper

Paprika and minced fresh parsley

Slice eggs in half lengthwise; remove yolks and set whites aside. In a small bowl, mash yolks with a fork. Add the mayonnaise, sugar, vinegar, mustard, salt and pepper. Stuff or pipe into egg whites. Garnish with paprika and parsley.

YIELD: 24 SERVINGS

Claudia Millhouse, Myersville, Maryland

My family doesn't like traditional deviled eggs, but they gobble up these sweet-sour versions. Our friends love them, too. The recipe yields 2 dozen, so I always have enough to bring to a potluck or party.

poppy seed rolls

Dottie Miller, Jonesborough, Tennessee

There's nothing like homemade rolls to round out a meal, and these are wonderful. Baked in muffin cups until they're golden brown, they complement just about every kind of main course and never disappoint at potlucks.

1 package (¼ ounce) active dry yeast

¼ cup warm water (110° to 115°)

¼ cup plus 1 teaspoon sugar, *divided*

1 cup warm milk (110° to 115°)

½ cup shortening

1½ teaspoons salt

1 egg, beaten

3¾ to 4 cups all-purpose flour

Butter, melted

Poppy seeds

1 In a mixing bowl, dissolve yeast in water. Add 1 teaspoon of sugar; let stand for 5 minutes. Beat in milk, shortening, salt, egg and remaining sugar. Add enough flour to form a soft dough.

2 Turn dough onto a floured surface; knead until smooth and elastic, about 6-8 minutes. Place in a greased bowl, turning once to grease top. Cover and let rise in a warm place until doubled, about 1 hour.

3 Punch the dough down. Divide into 18 portions; shape into balls. Place in greased muffin cups. Cover and let rise until doubled, about 30 minutes. Brush tops with butter; sprinkle with poppy seeds. Bake at 375° for 11-13 minutes or until golden brown. Remove from pans to wire racks.

YIELD: 1½ DOZEN

chocolate peanut butter cookies

2 cups butter

¼ cup shortening

2 cups baking cocoa

1 cup chocolate syrup

½ cup peanut butter

6 eggs

5 cups sugar

5 teaspoons vanilla extract

5 cups all-purpose flour

3 teaspoons baking soda

1 teaspoon salt

FILLING:

½ cup butter, softened

1 cup chunky peanut butter

1 cup milk

2 teaspoons vanilla extract

11 cups confectioners' sugar

1 In a saucepan over low heat, melt butter and shortening. Remove from the heat; stir in cocoa, chocolate syrup and peanut butter until smooth. Cool.

2 In a large mixing bowl, beat eggs and sugar until lemon-colored. Beat in the chocolate mixture and vanilla. Combine the flour, baking soda and salt; gradually add to creamed mixture. Drop by teaspoonfuls 2 in. apart onto ungreased baking sheets. Flatten with a glass dipped in sugar. Bake at 350° for 10-12 minutes or until surface cracks. Cool for 2 minutes before removing to wire racks.

3 In a mixing bowl, beat butter and peanut butter. Beat in milk and vanilla. Gradually add confectioners' sugar, beating until blended. Spread on the bottom of half of the cookies; top with remaining cookies.

YIELD: 11 DOZEN

Vickie Rhoads, Eugene, Oregon

Sandwich cookies are always a hit, and these homemade ones featuring peanut butter and chocolate are guaranteed to please. Whenever we visit out-of-town friends, they ask if we'll bring a batch of these memorable cookies.

roast beef roll-ups

½ cup sour cream

¼ cup mayonnaise

¼ cup salsa

10 flour tortillas (8 inches)

1 pound thinly sliced cooked roast beef

10 large lettuce leaves

Additional salsa

Combine sour cream, mayonnaise and salsa; spread over tortillas. Top with roast beef and lettuce. Roll up tightly and secure with toothpicks; cut in half. Serve with salsa.

YIELD: 10 SERVINGS

Susan Scott, Asheville, North Carolina

It's hard to believe that these delicious tortilla sandwiches jazzed up with salsa take mere moments to prepare. The satisfying roll-ups are great as a cool main dish on hot summer days...and even as a quick homemade lunch.

chive-cheese corn bread

Sybil Eades, Gainesville, Georgia

Not your "ordinary" corn bread, this version gets special flavor from chives and sharp cheddar cheese. I use a 13-in. x 9-in. pan for baking, then cut the bread into strips to feed a hungry crowd at a potluck or party.

1 cup cornmeal

1 cup all-purpose flour

¼ cup sugar

4 teaspoons baking powder

2 eggs

1 cup milk

¼ cup butter, melted

1 cup (4 ounces) shredded sharp cheddar cheese

3 tablespoons minced chives

1 In a large bowl, combine cornmeal, flour, sugar and baking powder. In another bowl, whisk the eggs, milk and butter. Stir into dry ingredients just until moistened. Gently fold in cheese and chives.

2 Pour into a greased 13-in. x 9-in. x 2-in. baking pan. Bake at 400° for 18 minutes or until golden brown. Cut into strips; serve warm.

YIELD: 12-15 SERVINGS

bundle up napkins and silverware

For your next potluck, consider wrapping each set of utensils in a large cloth or paper napkin. These all-in-one bundles are easy for guests to grab and carry.

Begin by folding the napkin into a square and lay it in front of you so it looks like a diamond shape. Place a set of utensils in the center of the napkin, leaving about a third of the napkin showing at the bottom. Fold the bottom corner up over the cutlery.

Fold the left side and then the right side of the napkin over the cutlery, tucking the right side underneath. Then secure the bundle by tying it with raffia or ribbon.

golden raisin oatmeal cookies

¾ cup butter, softened

1 cup packed brown sugar

½ cup sugar

1 egg

2 tablespoons water

1 teaspoon vanilla extract

3 cups quick-cooking oats

⅔ cup all-purpose flour

2 tablespoons grated orange peel

1 teaspoon ground cinnamon

½ teaspoon baking soda

⅔ cup golden raisins

1 In a mixing bowl, cream butter and sugars. Beat in egg, water and vanilla. Combine the oats, flour, orange peel, cinnamon and baking soda; gradually add to the creamed mixture. Stir in the raisins (dough will be stiff).

2 Drop dough by level tablespoonfuls 2 in. apart onto ungreased baking sheets. Bake at 350° for 12-15 minutes or until the edges are lightly browned. Remove to wire racks to cool.

YIELD: 4 DOZEN

Marion Lowery, Medford, Oregon

Here's a slightly different twist on a traditional favorite. These crisp, chewy oatmeal cookies feature golden raisins and have a mild orange tang. They're a popular choice when I need treats for a potluck or picnic.

super italian sub

1 loaf (1 pound) unsliced Italian
   bread

1/3 cup olive oil

1/4 cup red wine vinegar

8 garlic cloves, minced

1 teaspoon dried oregano

1/4 teaspoon pepper

1/2 pound thinly sliced fully cooked
   ham

1/2 pound thinly sliced cooked turkey

1/4 pound thinly sliced salami

1/4 pound sliced provolone cheese

1/4 pound sliced mozzarella cheese

1 medium green pepper, thinly sliced
   into rings

1 Cut bread in half lengthwise; hollow out top and bottom, leaving a
   1/2 -in. shell (discard removed bread or save for another use). Combine
   oil, vinegar, garlic, oregano and pepper; brush on cut sides of bread
   top and bottom.

2 On the bottom half of bread, layer half of the meats, cheeses and
   green pepper. Repeat layers. Replace bread top. Wrap tightly in plastic
   wrap; refrigerate for up to 24 hours.

YIELD: 10-12 SERVINGS

Patricia Lomp, Middleboro, Massachusetts

I love recipes that can be prepared ahead of time, and this sandwich offers me
that convenience. I just wrap the sub tightly in plastic wrap and keep it in the
refrigerator. At mealtime, all that's left to do is slice and enjoy.

garden focaccia

Mary Ann Ludwig, Edwardsville, Illinois

Frozen bread dough is the convenient starting point for this herb-flavored flat Italian bread. Topped with cheese and a variety of fresh veggies, these savory slices are satisfying enough to present as a meatless main dish.

1 loaf (1 pound) frozen bread dough, thawed

1 tablespoon olive oil

1 tablespoon minced fresh rosemary *or* 1 teaspoon dried rosemary, crushed

1 tablespoon minced fresh thyme *or* 1 teaspoon dried thyme

1 package (8 ounces) cream cheese, softened

¼ cup finely chopped onion

1 garlic clove, minced

4 large fresh mushrooms, sliced

3 medium tomatoes, sliced

1 small zucchini, thinly sliced

¼ cup grated Parmesan cheese

1 On a lightly floured surface, roll dough into a 15-in. x 10-in. rectangle. Place in a greased 15-in. x 10-in. x 1-in. baking pan. Cover and let rise for 30 minutes.

2 Using your fingertips, press indentations into the dough. Brush with oil; sprinkle with rosemary and thyme. Bake at 400° for 12-15 minutes or until golden brown. Cool slightly.

3 In a mixing bowl, combine cream cheese, onion and garlic. Spread over crust. Top with mushrooms, tomatoes and zucchini; sprinkle with Parmesan cheese. Bake for 12-15 minutes or until lightly browned. Cool for 5 minutes before cutting.

YIELD: 20 SLICES

garlic cheese biscuits

2 cups all-purpose flour

3 teaspoons garlic powder, *divided*

2½ teaspoons baking powder

½ teaspoon baking soda

1 teaspoon chicken bouillon
   granules

½ cup butter-flavored shortening

¾ cup shredded cheddar cheese

1 cup buttermilk

3 tablespoons butter, melted

1 In a small bowl, combine flour, 2 teaspoons garlic powder, baking powder, baking soda and bouillon; cut in shortening until mixture is crumbly. Add cheese. Stir in buttermilk just until moistened.

2 Drop by heaping tablespoonfuls 1 in. apart onto a greased baking sheet. Bake at 450° for 10 minutes. Combine butter and remaining garlic powder; brush over biscuits. Bake 4 minutes longer or until golden brown. Serve warm.

YIELD: ABOUT 1 DOZEN

Gayle Becker, Mt. Clemens, Michigan

This is a savory variation of my favorite buttermilk biscuit recipe. Shredded cheddar cheese adds attractive color to these drop biscuits, and they get extra flavor from the garlic-butter mixture I brush on top.

super brownies

½ cup butter

1½ cups sugar

4⅔ cups (28 ounces) semisweet chocolate chips, *divided*

3 tablespoons hot water

4 eggs

5 teaspoons vanilla extract

1½ cups all-purpose flour

½ teaspoon baking soda

½ teaspoon salt

2 cups coarsely chopped macadamia nuts *or* pecans, *divided*

1 In a saucepan over medium heat, melt butter and sugar. Remove from the heat; stir in 2 cups chocolate chips until melted. Pour into a mixing bowl; beat in water. Add eggs, one at a time, beating well after each addition. Add vanilla.

2 Combine flour, baking soda and salt; beat into the chocolate mixture until smooth. Stir in 2 cups of chocolate chips and 1 cup of nuts. Pour into a greased 13-in. x 9-in. x 2-in. baking pan. Sprinkle with remaining chips and nuts. Bake at 325° for 55 minutes or until the center is set (do not overbake).

YIELD: ABOUT 3½ DOZEN

Bernice Muilenburg, Molalla, Oregon

Loaded with chocolate chips and chopped macadamia nuts, these chunky treats never fail to catch attention on a potluck table...and to get snatched up by guests. If you prefer, replace the macadamia nuts with pecans.

creamy guacamole

Phyllis Allan, Vero Beach, Florida

As a transplanted New Englander, I was anxious to use some of Florida's fresh fruits in new recipes. This one quickly became a favorite. In fact, you may want to double it because the guacamole gets scooped up fast.

1 medium ripe avocado, halved, seeded and peeled

2 teaspoons lime juice

2 packages (3 ounces *each*) cream cheese, softened

1/2 teaspoon Worcestershire sauce

1/4 teaspoon salt

1/4 teaspoon hot pepper sauce

Tortilla chips

In a small mixing bowl, beat avocado with lime juice. Add the cream cheese, Worcestershire sauce, salt and hot pepper sauce; beat until smooth. Serve with tortilla chips. Store in the refrigerator.

YIELD: 1 1/3 CUPS

prepare a pepper cup for dip

Whether red, green, yellow or orange, a sweet bell pepper makes a bright and attractive serving dish for a creamy dip. To create a pepper cup, use a sharp knife to cut the stem and about 1/2 inch off the top of the pepper. Carefully remove the membrane and seeds inside.

If necessary, cut a thin slice off the bottom of the pepper so it sits flat. You could also give it a decorative design by cutting out triangle shapes along the top edge. When you've finished cutting, fill the cup with dip.

cherry bars

1 cup butter, softened

2 cups sugar

4 eggs

1 teaspoon vanilla extract

¼ teaspoon almond extract

3 cups all-purpose flour

1 teaspoon salt

2 cans (21 ounces *each*) cherry
  pie filling

GLAZE:

1 cup confectioners' sugar

½ teaspoon vanilla extract

½ teaspoon almond extract

2 to 3 tablespoons milk

1 In a large mixing bowl, cream butter and sugar. Add eggs, one at a time, beating well after each addition. Beat in the extracts. Combine flour and salt; add to the creamed mixture and mix until combined.

2 Spread 3 cups batter into a greased 15-in. x 10-in. x 1-in. baking pan. Spread with pie filling. Drop the remaining batter by teaspoonfuls over filling. Bake at 350° for 30-35 minutes or until a toothpick comes out clean. Cool on wire rack. Combine glaze ingredients; drizzle over bars.

YIELD: 5 DOZEN

Jane Kamp, Grand Rapids, Michigan

Looking for something simple but special to bring to your next potluck? Try these tempting fruit-filled bars. They get gorgeous ruby-red color from cherry pie filling and also boast subtle almond flavor.

caramel chocolate cheesecake bites

¾ cup toasted wheat germ

2 packages (8 ounces *each*) cream cheese

¾ cup sugar

⅓ cup baking cocoa

4 egg whites

1 teaspoon vanilla extract

36 pecan halves

3 tablespoons caramel ice cream topping

1 Coat 36 miniature muffin cups with nonstick cooking spray; generously coat each with wheat germ. Set aside. In a mixing bowl, beat cream cheese and sugar until smooth. Add cocoa; mix well. Beat in egg whites and vanilla just until combined.

2 Spoon 4 teaspoons into each muffin cup. Bake at 350° for 13-16 minutes or until set. Cool in pans for 10 minutes before removing to wire racks. Cool for 30 minutes and refrigerate. (Cheesecakes may sink in the center upon cooling.)

3 To serve, top each with a pecan half. Microwave caramel topping on high for 10 seconds or until soft. Spoon ¼ teaspoon over each.

YIELD: 3 DOZEN

Barbara Nowakowski, North Tonawanda, New York

These tantalizing treats are the perfect size for people who like to sample different desserts at potlucks. Baked in mini muffin cups, the caramel- and pecan-topped bites offer a satisfying taste of rich chocolate cheesecake.

colorful crab appetizer pizza

Diane Caron, Des Moines, Iowa

If you want something easy-but-special for a potluck, try this recipe. It's a fresh-tasting and attractive variation of a cold vegetable pizza. I make it as an appetizer for parties all the time...and even as a light main dish with a soup or salad.

1 tube (8 ounces) refrigerated crescent rolls

1 package (8 ounces) cream cheese, softened

1½ cups coarsely chopped fresh spinach, *divided*

1 green onion, thinly sliced

1½ teaspoons minced fresh dill *or* ½ teaspoon dill weed

1 teaspoon grated lemon peel, *divided*

½ teaspoon lemon juice

⅛ teaspoon pepper

1¼ cups chopped imitation crabmeat

¼ cup chopped ripe olives

1 Unroll crescent roll dough and place on an ungreased 12-in. pizza pan. Flatten dough, sealing seams and perforations. Bake at 350° for 8-10 minutes or until lightly browned; cool.

2 In a small mixing bowl, beat cream cheese until smooth. Stir in 1 cup spinach, onion, dill, ½ teaspoon lemon peel, lemon juice and pepper. Spread over the crust. Top with crab, olives and remaining spinach and lemon peel. Cut into bite-size squares.

YIELD: 8-10 SERVINGS

fried cinnamon strips

1 cup sugar

1 teaspoon ground cinnamon

¼ teaspoon ground nutmeg

10 flour tortillas (8 inches)

Vegetable oil

1 In a large resealable plastic bag, combine sugar, cinnamon and nutmeg; set aside. Cut tortillas into 3-in. x 2-in. strips. Heat 1 in. of oil in a skillet or electric fry pan to 375°; fry 4-5 strips at a time for 30 seconds on each side or until golden brown. Drain on paper towels.

2 While still warm, place strips in bag with sugar mixture; shake gently to coat. Serve immediately or store in an airtight container.

YIELD: 5 DOZEN

Nancy Johnson, Laverne, Oklahoma

The first time I prepared these crispy strips for a gathering, most of them were snatched up before dinner! Fried and then coated with spices and sugar, these change-of-pace chips always prove irresistible.

hot artichoke spread

1 can (14 ounces) water-packed artichoke hearts, drained and chopped

1 cup mayonnaise

1 cup grated Parmesan cheese

1 can (4 ounces) chopped green chilies, drained

1 garlic clove, minced

1 cup chopped fresh tomatoes

3 green onions, thinly sliced

Crackers *or* pita bread

In a bowl, combine the first five ingredients. Spread into a 1-qt. baking dish or 9-in. pie plate. Bake, uncovered, at 350° for 20-25 minutes or until top is lightly browned. Sprinkle with tomatoes and onions. Serve with crackers or pita bread.

YIELD: 4½ CUPS

EDITOR'S NOTE: Reduced-fat or fat-free mayonnaise may not be substituted for regular mayonnaise.

Victoria Casey, Coeur d'Alene, Idaho

Green chilies add a bit of zip to this rich, cheesy spread topped with colorful tomatoes and onions. I prepare it often because it's not only delicious, it's also easy to make. Serve it with your favorite crackers or pita bread.

dishes in a hurry

124

132

Who has time to spend hours preparing for a potluck? The good news is, you don't have to rearrange your busy schedule to bring a delicious, impressive, feed-a-crowd dish. It's mere minutes away when you pick from the rave-review recipes in this chapter.

In fact, each of these outstanding foods is ready to serve in just 1 hour—or less. That means you'll need only a little time in the kitchen before you can serve fabulous fare like Crunchy Asparagus Medley (p. 124) and Italian Meatball Hoagies (p. 132).

layered ham and spinach salad

Beverly Sprague, Baltimore, Maryland

Swiss cheese, chopped eggs and bacon make this layered ham salad an even heartier dish. Not only does it look impressive on a potluck table, it's also easy to assemble. I spread ranch salad dressing on top for great flavor.

16 cups torn fresh spinach

1 teaspoon sugar

1 teaspoon pepper

¼ teaspoon salt

6 hard-cooked eggs, chopped

1½ cups cubed fully cooked ham

1 medium red onion, sliced

1 envelope ranch salad dressing mix

1½ cups mayonnaise

1 cup (8 ounces) sour cream

2 cups (8 ounces) shredded Swiss cheese

½ pound sliced bacon, cooked and crumbled

1 Place two-thirds of the spinach in a 4-qt. salad bowl. Sprinkle with half of the sugar, pepper and salt. Top with eggs, ham and remaining spinach. Sprinkle with remaining sugar, pepper and salt. Arrange onion slices on top.

2 In a bowl, combine the dressing mix, mayonnaise and sour cream. Spread over onions. Sprinkle with cheese and bacon. Refrigerate until serving.

YIELD: 8-10 SERVINGS

cappuccino mousse trifle

2½ cups cold milk

⅓ cup instant coffee granules

2 packages (3.4 ounces *each*) instant vanilla pudding mix

1 carton (16 ounces) frozen whipped topping, thawed, *divided*

2 loaves (10¾ ounces *each*) frozen pound cake, thawed and cubed

1 square (1 ounce) semisweet chocolate, grated

¼ teaspoon ground cinnamon

1 In a mixing bowl, stir the milk and coffee granules until dissolved; remove 1 cup and set aside. Add pudding mixes to the remaining milk mixture; beat on low speed for 2 minutes or until thickened. Fold in half of the whipped topping.

2 Place a third of the cake cubes in a 4-qt. serving or trifle bowl; layer with a third of the reserved milk mixture and pudding mixture and a fourth of the grated chocolate. Repeat layers twice. Garnish with remaining whipped topping and chocolate. Sprinkle with cinnamon. Cover and refrigerate until serving.

YIELD: 16-20 SERVINGS

Tracy Bergland, Prior Lake, Minnesota

This is the easiest trifle I've ever made, yet it looks like I spent hours preparing it. I sometimes pipe whipped topping around the edge of the bowl and grate chocolate in the center. It always gets rave reviews.

apple-cherry cobbler

1 egg, beaten

1/2 cup sugar

1/2 cup milk

2 tablespoons vegetable oil

1 cup all-purpose flour

2 1/4 teaspoons baking powder

1 can (21 ounces) apple pie filling

1 can (21 ounces) cherry pie filling

1 tablespoon lemon juice

1 teaspoon vanilla extract

TOPPING:

1/3 cup packed brown sugar

3 tablespoons all-purpose flour

2 tablespoons butter, softened

1 teaspoon ground cinnamon

Whipped cream, optional

1 In a bowl, combine the first four ingredients. Combine flour and baking powder; add to egg mixture and blend well. Pour into a greased 13-in. x 9-in. x 2-in. baking pan. Combine pie fillings, lemon juice and vanilla; spoon over batter.

2 For topping, combine all ingredients; sprinkle over filling. Bake at 350° for 40-45 minutes or until bubbly and a toothpick comes out clean. If necessary, cover edges with foil to prevent over-browning. Serve with whipped cream if desired.

YIELD: 12-16 SERVINGS

Eleanore Hill, Fresno, California

With an out-of-the-ordinary combination of fruits, this cobbler recipe gives a traditional dessert a tempting twist. People of all ages appreciate this old-fashioned comfort food, especially when I top it with whipped cream.

nutty broccoli slaw

Dora Clapsaddle, Kensington, Ohio

My daughter gave me the recipe for this fantastic salad. The sweet dressing nicely coats a crisp blend of broccoli slaw mix, carrots, onions, almonds and sunflower kernels. Crushed ramen noodles provide even more crunch. It's a smash hit wherever I take it.

1 package (3 ounces) chicken ramen noodles

1 package (16 ounces) broccoli slaw mix

2 cups sliced green onions (about 2 bunches)

1½ cups broccoli florets

1 can (6 ounces) ripe olives, drained and halved

1 cup sunflower kernels, toasted

½ cup slivered almonds, toasted

½ cup sugar

½ cup cider vinegar

½ cup olive oil

1 Set aside the noodle seasoning packet; crush the noodles and place in a large bowl. Add the slaw mix, onions, broccoli, olives, sunflower kernels and almonds.

2 In a jar with a tight-fitting lid, combine the sugar, vinegar, oil and contents of seasoning packet; shake well. Drizzle over salad and toss to coat. Serve immediately.

YIELD: 16 SERVINGS

crunchy asparagus medley

1½ pounds fresh asparagus, cut
   into 2-inch pieces

1 cup thinly sliced celery

2 cans (8 ounces *each*) sliced water
   chestnuts, drained

¼ cup slivered almonds, toasted

2 tablespoons soy sauce

2 tablespoons butter

In a large saucepan, cook the asparagus and celery in a small amount of water for 5-6 minutes or until crisp-tender; drain. Stir in the water chestnuts, almonds, soy sauce and butter; heat through.

YIELD: 8-10 SERVINGS

Mary Gaylord, Balsam Lake, Wisconsin

With celery, water chestnuts and toasted almonds, this recipe really lives up to its "crunchy" name! I've prepared the savory side dish for many get-togethers, including a Hawaiian-theme dinner I hosted for family and friends.

tasty reuben soup

4 cans (14½ ounces *each*) chicken broth

4 cups shredded cabbage

2 cups uncooked medium egg noodles

1 pound fully cooked kielbasa *or* Polish sausage, halved and cut into 1-inch slices

½ cup chopped onion

1 teaspoon caraway seeds

¼ teaspoon garlic powder

1 cup (4 ounces) shredded Swiss cheese

In a large saucepan, combine the first seven ingredients; bring to a boil. Reduce heat; cover and simmer for 15 minutes or until cabbage and noodles are tender. Garnish with cheese.

YIELD: 10 SERVINGS (2½ QUARTS)

Terry Ann Brandt, Tobias, Nebraska

I'm a working mom with limited time to spend in the kitchen, so I'm always looking for quick and easy recipes. With the flavor of a Reuben sandwich, this delicious noodle soup gets rave reviews from everyone who tries it.

calico potato salad

DRESSING:

1/2 cup olive oil

1/4 cup vinegar

1 tablespoon sugar

1 1/2 teaspoons chili powder

1 teaspoon salt, optional

Dash hot pepper sauce

SALAD:

4 large red potatoes (about 2 pounds), peeled and cooked

1 1/2 cups cooked whole kernel corn

1 cup shredded carrot

1/2 cup chopped red onion

1/2 cup diced green pepper

1/2 cup diced sweet red pepper

1/2 cup sliced pitted ripe olives

In a small bowl or jar, combine all dressing ingredients; cover and chill. Cube potatoes; combine with corn, carrot, onion, peppers and olives in a salad bowl. Pour dressing over; toss lightly. Cover and chill.

YIELD: 14 SERVINGS

Christine Hartry, Emo, Ontario

One of the best things about this dish is how versatile it is. I've taken the colorful salad to many different types of gatherings, and it goes well with a variety of meats. Chili powder and hot pepper sauce give it a little kick.

refreshing lemon-lime drink

Lisa Castillo, Bourbonnais, Illinois

Here's a refreshing version of the popular margarita—without the alcohol. Bursting with a tangy blend of lemon and lime, this beverage is perfect for get-togethers on hot summer days and goes wonderfully with Mexican food.

1 can (12 ounces) frozen limeade concentrate, thawed

2/3 cup frozen lemonade concentrate, thawed

1 teaspoon orange extract

1 1/2 cups water

6 cups chilled lemon-lime soda

1 medium lemon, sliced

1 medium lime, sliced

In a large container, combine the limeade and lemonade concentrates and orange extract. Stir in water. Just before serving, stir in lemon-lime soda. Serve over ice. Garnish with lemon and lime slices.

YIELD: 3 QUARTS

put thirst-quenchers on flavorful ice

Beverages that are kept cold with ordinary ice cubes or ice rings become watered down as the ice melts. To keep your punch or other drink at its flavorful best, simply fill the ring mold or ice cube trays with a portion of your punch instead of water. For extra flair, freeze strawberries, raspberries, grapes, sliced peaches or other fruit inside the cubes or ring.

black forest brownies

1 1/3 cups all-purpose flour

1 teaspoon baking powder

1/2 teaspoon salt

1 cup butter

1 cup baking cocoa

4 eggs, beaten

2 cups sugar

1 1/2 teaspoons vanilla extract

1 teaspoon almond extract

1 cup chopped maraschino cherries

1/2 cup chopped nuts

ICING:

1/4 cup butter, softened

1 teaspoon vanilla extract

2 cups confectioners' sugar

6 tablespoons baking cocoa

1/4 cup milk

1/4 cup chopped nuts

1 Combine flour, baking powder and salt; set aside. In a large saucepan, melt butter. Remove from the heat and stir in cocoa until smooth. Blend in eggs, sugar and extracts. Stir in flour mixture, cherries and nuts. Pour into a greased 13-in. x 9-in. x 2-in. baking pan. Bake at 350° for 35 minutes or until a toothpick inserted near the center comes out clean.

2 For icing, blend butter, vanilla, sugar, cocoa and milk until smooth; spread over warm brownies. Sprinkle with nuts. Cool.

YIELD: 3 DOZEN

Toni Reeves, Medicine Hat, Alberta

You can spread the chocolate icing on these cherry-filled treats while they're still warm from the oven. For the finishing touch, just sprinkle on nuts.

chewy pecan pie bars

¼ cup butter, melted

2 cups packed brown sugar

⅔ cup all-purpose flour

4 eggs

2 teaspoons vanilla extract

¼ teaspoon baking soda

¼ teaspoon salt

2 cups chopped pecans

Confectioners' sugar

1 Pour butter into a 13-in. x 9-in. x 2-in. baking pan; set aside. In a mixing bowl, combine brown sugar, flour, eggs, vanilla, baking soda and salt; mix well. Stir in pecans. Spread over butter.

2 Bake at 350° for 30-35 minutes. Remove from the oven; immediately dust with confectioners' sugar. Cool before cutting.

YIELD: ABOUT 2 DOZEN

Judy Taylor, Shreveport, Louisiana

One of my husband's favorites, this recipe gives you all the goodness of pecan pie in easy-to-serve bars. I like to dust them with confectioners' sugar.

shrimp appetizer spread

Brenda Buhler, Abbotsford, British Columbia

When I first tasted this sensational seafood appetizer at a friend's house, I had to have the recipe. The colorful spread looks impressive on a buffet table but actually requires little time and effort in the kitchen.

1 package (8 ounces) cream cheese, softened

½ cup sour cream

¼ cup mayonnaise

3 packages (5 ounces *each*) frozen cooked salad shrimp, thawed

1 cup seafood sauce

2 cups (8 ounces) shredded mozzarella cheese

1 medium green pepper, chopped

1 small tomato, chopped

3 green onions with tops, sliced

Assorted crackers

1 In a mixing bowl, beat cream cheese until smooth. Add sour cream and mayonnaise; mix well. Spread mixture on a round 12-in. serving platter.

2 Sprinkle mixture with shrimp. Top with seafood sauce. Sprinkle with mozzarella cheese, green pepper, tomato and onions. Cover and refrigerate. Serve with crackers.

YIELD: 20 SERVINGS

ricotta pepperoni dip

1 tube (10 ounces) refrigerated pizza crust

1 tablespoon olive oil

2 tablespoons grated Parmesan cheese

1 tablespoon Italian seasoning

¼ teaspoon garlic powder

⅛ teaspoon pepper

DIP:

1 cup (8 ounces) sour cream

1 cup ricotta cheese

1 tablespoon savory herb with garlic soup mix

¼ cup chopped pepperoni

1 cup (4 ounces) shredded mozzarella cheese

1 tablespoon grated Parmesan cheese

1 On a lightly floured surface, roll out pizza crust to a 12-in. x 8 in. rectangle. Brush with oil. Combine the Parmesan cheese, Italian seasoning, garlic powder and pepper; sprinkle over dough. Cut into 3-in. x 1-in. strips; place on a greased baking sheet. Bake at 425° for 6-9 minutes or until golden brown.

2 Meanwhile, combine the sour cream, ricotta, soup mix and pepperoni in a saucepan; heat through. Stir in mozzarella and Parmesan cheeses just until melted. Serve warm with pizza sticks.

YIELD: ABOUT 2½ DOZEN PIZZA STICKS AND 2 CUPS DIP

Barbara Carlucci, Orange Park, Florida

Using convenient refrigerated pizza crust, I can quickly prepare seasoned, golden brown breadsticks to serve with this warm dip. Herb-and-garlic soup mix, chopped pepperoni and three kinds of cheese give it fantastic flavor.

angel rolls

3½ cups bread flour, *divided*

2 tablespoons sugar

1 package (¼ ounce) quick-rise yeast

1¼ teaspoons salt

1 teaspoon baking powder

½ teaspoon baking soda

1 cup warm buttermilk (120° to 130°)

½ cup vegetable oil

⅓ cup warm water (120° to 130°)

Melted butter

1 In a mixing bowl, combine 1½ cups flour, sugar, yeast, salt, baking powder and baking soda. Add the buttermilk, oil and water; beat until moistened. Stir in enough remaining flour to form a soft dough. Turn onto a floured surface and knead until smooth and elastic, about 4-6 minutes. Cover and let rest for 10 minutes.

2 Roll out to ½-in. thickness; cut with a 2½-in. biscuit cutter. Place on a greased baking sheet. Bake at 400° for 15-18 minutes or until golden brown. Brush tops with butter.

YIELD: 14 ROLLS

EDITOR'S NOTE: Warm buttermilk will appear curdled.

Debbie Graber, Eureka, Nevada
Thanks to this quick-rise yeast recipe, I can offer family and friends the unbeatable goodness of homemade rolls without spending a lot of time in the kitchen. They're soft, tender and always a crowd-pleaser at potlucks.

lemon cheesecake squares

Peggy Reddick, Cumming, Georgia

Here's a wonderful way to serve cheesecake to a crowd. Whether I'm hosting friends or attending a potluck, these creamy, elegant squares are a guaranteed hit. I also like the fact that I can make them ahead of time if needed.

¾ cup shortening

⅓ cup packed brown sugar

1¼ cups all-purpose flour

1 cup rolled oats

¼ teaspoon salt

½ cup seedless raspberry jam

FILLING:

4 packages (8 ounces *each*) cream cheese, softened

1½ cups sugar

¼ cup all-purpose flour

4 eggs

⅓ cup lemon juice

4 teaspoons grated lemon peel

1 In a mixing bowl, cream shortening and brown sugar. Combine the flour, oats and salt; gradually add to creamed mixture. Press dough into a greased 13-in. x 9-in. x 2-in. baking dish. Bake at 350° for 15-18 minutes or until golden brown. Spread with jam.

2 For filling, beat the cream cheese, sugar and flour until fluffy. Add the eggs, lemon juice and peel just until blended. Carefully spoon over jam. Bake at 350° for 30-35 minutes or until center is almost set. Cool on a wire rack. Cover and store in the refrigerator.

YIELD: 20 SERVINGS

Morning potlucks bring their own unique array of delicious dish options. From individual Cheesy Egg Puffs (p. 174) to creamy Strawberry Yogurt Crunch (p. 170), the early-day recipes featured in this chapter will shine on any breakfast or brunch table.

You'll find that all of these crowd-favorite foods can either be started the night before or easily assembled the morning of the potluck. So you won't have to rise at the crack of dawn to prepare and share a day-brightening dish with friends and family.

blueberry oat muffins

Mildred Mummau, Mt. Joy, Pennsylvania

Bursting with blueberries and hearty oats, these tender muffins also get a touch of spice and extra sweetness from the cinnamon-sugar topping I add just before baking. These treats never last long when you present them at a potluck or serve them for a family breakfast.

1¼ cups all-purpose flour

1 cup quick-cooking oats

½ cup sugar

1 teaspoon baking powder

½ teaspoon baking soda

¼ teaspoon salt

2 egg whites

½ cup water

⅓ cup vegetable oil

1 cup fresh *or* frozen blueberries

TOPPING:

2 tablespoons sugar

¼ teaspoon ground cinnamon

1 In a bowl, combine the first six ingredients. In another bowl, beat egg whites, water and oil. Stir into dry ingredients just until moistened. Fold in blueberries. Fill paper-lined muffin cups or muffin cups coated with nonstick cooking spray three-fourths full.

2 Combine sugar and cinnamon; sprinkle over muffins. Bake at 400° for 18-22 minutes or until a toothpick comes out clean. Cool for 5 minutes before removing from pan to a wire rack.

YIELD: 1 DOZEN

EDITOR'S NOTE: If using frozen blueberries, do not thaw before adding to the batter.

no-knead citrus rolls

¼ cup warm water (110° to 115°)

2 packages (¼ ounce *each*) active dry yeast

7 tablespoons sugar, *divided*

1 cup warm heavy whipping cream (110° to 115°)

3 egg yolks, beaten

3½ to 4 cups all-purpose flour

1 teaspoon salt

¾ cup cold butter, *divided*

FILLING:

½ cup sugar

2 tablespoons grated lemon peel

2 tablespoons grated orange peel

GLAZE:

1⅓ cups confectioners' sugar

2 tablespoons milk

1 tablespoon lemon juice

1 tablespoon orange juice

1 In a bowl, combine water, yeast and 1 tablespoon sugar. Let stand 5 minutes. Stir in cream and egg yolks; mix well. In another bowl, combine 3½ cups flour, salt and remaining sugar; cut in ½ cup butter until crumbly. Add yeast mixture; stir just until moistened. Add enough remaining flour to form a soft dough. Place in a greased bowl, turning once to grease top. Refrigerate for 6-8 hours or overnight.

2 Punch dough down. Turn onto a lightly floured surface. Divide in half; roll each into a 15-in. x 12-in. rectangle. Melt remaining butter; brush over dough. Combine filling ingredients; sprinkle over dough. Roll up, jelly-roll style, beginning with a long side; pinch seam to seal.

3 Cut each roll into 15 slices; place cut side down in two greased 9-in. pie plates. Cover and let rise until doubled, about 45 minutes. Bake at 375° for 20-25 minutes or until golden brown. Combine glaze ingredients; drizzle over warm rolls. Cool in pans on wire racks.

YIELD: 2½ DOZEN

Margaret Otley, Waverly, Nebraska

With a sweet filling and flaky texture, these orange- and lemon-flavored treats have homemade goodness but don't require the extra step of kneading. I like that I can prepare the dough the night before. In the morning, I just fill and shape the rolls, then pop them in the oven and drizzle on the citrusy glaze.

sausage hash brown bake

2 pounds bulk pork sausage

2 cups (8 ounces) shredded cheddar cheese, *divided*

1 can (10¾ ounces) condensed cream of chicken soup, undiluted

1 cup (8 ounces) sour cream

1 carton (8 ounces) French onion dip

1 cup chopped onion

¼ cup chopped green pepper

¼ cup chopped sweet red pepper

⅛ teaspoon pepper

1 package (30 ounces) frozen shredded hash brown potatoes, thawed

1 In a large skillet, cook sausage over medium heat until no longer pink; drain on paper towels. In a large bowl, combine 1¾ cups cheese and the next seven ingredients; fold in potatoes.

2 Spread half of potato mixture into a greased shallow 3-qt. baking dish. Top with sausage and remaining potato mixture. Sprinkle with remaining cheese. Cover and bake at 350° for 45 minutes. Uncover; bake 10 minutes longer or until heated through.

YIELD: 10-12 SERVINGS

Esther Wrinkles, Vanzant, Missouri

For this all-in-one breakfast casserole, I sandwich pork sausage between layers of hash browns flavored with cream soup and French onion dip. Cheddar cheese completes this colorful and satisfying dish.

sticky bun coffee ring

Viola Shephard, Bay City, Michigan

Everyone thinks I went to a lot of trouble when I bring out this pretty nut-topped ring of scrumptious caramel rolls. In fact, these tasty treats are easy to put together using refrigerated biscuits. They're best when warm and chewy.

3 tablespoons butter, melted, *divided*

3 tablespoons maple syrup

¼ cup packed brown sugar

¼ cup chopped pecans

¼ cup chopped almonds

½ teaspoon ground cinnamon

1 tube (12 ounces) refrigerated buttermilk biscuits

1 Brush a 10-in. fluted tube pan with 1 tablespoon butter. In a small bowl, combine syrup and remaining butter. Drizzle 2 tablespoons into pan. Combine brown sugar, nuts and cinnamon; sprinkle ⅓ cupful over syrup mixture.

2 Separate biscuits; place in prepared pan with edges overlapping. Top with remaining syrup and nut mixtures. Bake at 375° for 15 minutes or until golden brown. Cool for 1-2 minutes; invert onto a serving platter. Serve warm.

YIELD: 10 SERVINGS

apple danish

PASTRY:

3 cups all-purpose flour

1/2 teaspoon salt

1 cup shortening

1 egg yolk

1/2 cup milk

FILLING:

6 cups sliced peeled apples

1 1/2 cups sugar

1/4 cup butter, melted

2 tablespoons all-purpose flour

1 teaspoon ground cinnamon

GLAZE:

1 egg white, lightly beaten

1/2 cup confectioners' sugar

2 to 3 teaspoons water

1 In a mixing bowl, combine flour and salt; cut in shortening until mixture resembles coarse crumbs. Combine egg yolk and milk; add to flour mixture. Stir just until dough clings together. Divide dough in half. On a lightly floured surface, roll half of dough into a 15-in. x 10-in. rectangle; transfer to a greased 15-in. x 10-in. x 1-in. baking pan. Set aside.

2 In a bowl, toss together filling ingredients; spoon over pastry in pan. Roll out remaining dough to another 15-in. x 10-in. rectangle. Place over filling. Brush with egg white. Bake at 375° for 40 minutes or until golden brown. Cool on a wire rack.

3 Combine the confectioners' sugar and enough water to achieve a drizzling consistency. Drizzle over warm pastry. Cut into squares. Serve warm or cold.

YIELD: 20-24 SERVINGS

Sandy Lynch, Decatur, Illinois

A friend gave me this recipe that makes good use of our bountiful apple harvest. The pastries are very moist and make a perfect addition to breakfast or brunch.

black forest crepes

1¼ cups buttermilk

3 eggs

3 tablespoons butter, melted

1 cup all-purpose flour

2 tablespoons sugar

2 tablespoons baking cocoa

CHOCOLATE SAUCE:

¾ cup sugar

⅓ cup baking cocoa

1 can (5 ounces) evaporated milk

¼ cup butter

1 teaspoon vanilla extract

1 can (21 ounces) cherry pie filling

1 In a mixing bowl, combine buttermilk, eggs and butter. Combine flour, sugar and cocoa; add to milk mixture and mix well. Cover and chill for 1 hour.

2 Heat a lightly greased 8-in. nonstick skillet; add 2 tablespoons batter. Lift and tilt pan to evenly coat bottom. Cook until top appears dry; turn and cook 15-20 seconds longer. Remove to a wire rack. Repeat with remaining batter. When cool, stack crepes with waxed paper or paper towels in between.

3 For sauce, combine sugar and cocoa in a saucepan. Whisk in milk; add butter. Bring to a boil over medium heat, stirring constantly. Remove from the heat; stir in vanilla.

4 To serve, spoon about 2 tablespoons pie filling down the center of each crepe. Fold sides of crepe over filling; place in a greased 13-in. x 9-in. x 2-in. baking pan. Bake, uncovered, at 225° for 15 minutes. Transfer to serving plates; drizzle with warm chocolate sauce.

YIELD: 10 SERVINGS (20 CREPES)

EDITOR'S NOTE: Unfilled crepes may be covered and refrigerated for 2 to 3 days or frozen for 4 months.

Lisa Tanner, Warner Robins, Georgia

These fancy-looking crepes baked in a 13-in. x 9-in. pan are a sweet ending to a special-occasion meal. I fill them with cherry pie filling and top them with chocolate sauce, whipped cream and a sprinkling of baking cocoa.

strawberry yogurt crunch

Becky Palac, Escondido, California

Yogurt is always a favorite breakfast choice, but this recipe transforms it into something special. With a nutty coconut crust and topping, this creamy-crunchy treat can even make a light dessert for afternoon or evening meals.

¾ cup butter, softened

⅓ cup packed brown sugar

½ cup all-purpose flour

½ teaspoon ground cinnamon

¼ teaspoon baking soda

1 cup quick-cooking oats

1 cup flaked coconut, toasted

⅓ cup chopped nuts

1 carton (8 ounces) frozen whipped topping, thawed

2 cartons (6 ounces *each*) strawberry custard-style yogurt *or* flavor of your choice

1 In a mixing bowl, cream butter and brown sugar. Combine the flour, cinnamon and baking soda; gradually add to creamed mixture. Stir in the oats, coconut and nuts. Remove 1 cup for topping. Press remaining oat mixture into an ungreased 13-in. x 9-in. x 2-in. baking dish. Bake at 350° for 12-13 minutes or until light brown. Cool on a wire rack.

2 In a bowl, fold whipped topping into yogurt. Spread over crust. Sprinkle with reserved oat mixture. Cover and refrigerate for 4 hours or overnight.

YIELD: 12-15 SERVINGS

brunch fruit salad

1 can (20 ounces) pineapple chunks

2 large firm bananas, cut into ¼ -inch chunks

1 cup green grapes

1 can (15 ounces) mandarin oranges, drained

1 Golden Delicious apple, sliced

1 Red Delicious apple, sliced

½ cup sugar

2 tablespoons cornstarch

⅓ cup orange juice

1 tablespoon lemon juice

1 Drain pineapple, reserving juice. Combine the pineapple chunks, bananas, grapes, mandarin oranges and sliced apples in a large bowl; set aside.

2 In a saucepan, combine sugar and cornstarch. Add the orange juice, lemon juice and reserved pineapple juice; stir until smooth. Bring to a boil; reduce heat. Cook and stir for 2 minutes. Pour over fruit; mix gently. Cover and refrigerate until serving.

YIELD: 10 SERVINGS

Millie Vickery, Lena, Illinois

I coat convenient canned and fresh fruits with a quick stovetop sauce to create this colorful salad. It's the perfect light accompaniment to egg bakes and other hearty breakfast casseroles, so it disappears quickly at morning potlucks.

butterscotch muffins

2 cups all-purpose flour

1 cup sugar

1 package (3.4 ounces) instant butterscotch pudding mix

1 package (3.4 ounces) instant vanilla pudding mix

2 teaspoons baking powder

1 teaspoon salt

1 cup water

4 eggs

3/4 cup vegetable oil

1 teaspoon vanilla extract

TOPPING:

2/3 cup packed brown sugar

1/2 cup chopped pecans

2 teaspoons ground cinnamon

1 In a bowl, combine the flour, sugar, pudding mixes, baking powder and salt. Combine the water, eggs, oil and vanilla; stir into the dry ingredients just until moistened. Fill greased or paper-lined muffin cups two-thirds full.

2 Combine the topping ingredients; sprinkle over batter. Bake at 350° for 15-20 minutes or until a toothpick comes out clean. Cool for 5 minutes before removing from pans to wire racks.

YIELD: ABOUT 1½ DOZEN

Jill Hazelton, Hamlet, Indiana

Butterscotch pudding gives a distinctive flavor to these tempting muffins topped with brown sugar, chopped pecans and cinnamon. My son prepared these treats for a 4-H competition, and they won first-place ribbons.

cheesy egg puffs

Amy Soto, Winfield, Kansas

My father loves to entertain, and these buttery egg delights are one of his favorite items to serve at brunch. The leftovers are perfect to reheat in the microwave on busy mornings, so Dad always stashes a few away for me to take home after the party is over.

½ pound fresh mushrooms, sliced

4 green onions, chopped

1 tablespoon plus ½ cup butter, *divided*

½ cup all-purpose flour

1 teaspoon baking powder

½ teaspoon salt

10 eggs, lightly beaten

4 cups (16 ounces) shredded Monterey Jack cheese

2 cups (16 ounces) small-curd cottage cheese

1 In a skillet, saute the mushrooms and onions in 1 tablespoon butter until tender. In a large bowl, combine the flour, baking powder and salt. In another bowl, combine eggs and cheeses. Melt remaining butter; add to egg mixture. Stir into dry ingredients along with mushroom mixture.

2 Fill greased muffin cups three-fourths full. Bake at 350° for 35-40 minutes or until a knife inserted near the center comes out clean. Carefully run the knife around edge of muffin cups before removing.

YIELD: 2½ DOZEN

put a spin on paper napkins

To dress up a stack of paper napkins, simply "swirl" it using a drinking glass or coffee mug. First, stack the napkins in a pile with even edges and lay the glass on its side on top.

Holding the glass firmly and pressing down on the stack, turn the glass slightly in a circular motion to begin fanning the napkins. You'll need to lift the glass and repeat this step several times to fan the napkins into a pretty swirl.

bacon 'n' egg lasagna

1 pound sliced bacon, diced

1 large onion, chopped

1/3 cup all-purpose flour

1/2 to 1 teaspoon salt

1/4 teaspoon pepper

4 cups milk

12 lasagna noodles, cooked and drained

12 hard-cooked eggs, sliced

2 cups (8 ounces) shredded Swiss cheese

1/3 cup grated Parmesan cheese

2 tablespoons minced fresh parsley

1 In a skillet, cook bacon until crisp. Remove with a slotted spoon to paper towels. Drain, reserving 1/3 cup drippings. In the drippings, saute onion until tender. Stir in flour, salt and pepper until blended. Gradually stir in milk. Bring to a boil; cook and stir for 2 minutes. Remove from the heat.

2 Spread 1/2 cup sauce in a greased 13-in. x 9-in. x 2-in. baking dish. Layer with four noodles, a third of the eggs and bacon, Swiss cheese and white sauce. Repeat layers twice. Sprinkle with Parmesan cheese. Bake, uncovered, at 350° for 35-40 minutes or until bubbly. Sprinkle with parsley. Let stand 15 minutes before cutting.

YIELD: 12 SERVINGS

Dianne Meyer, Graniteville, Vermont

My sister-in-law served this special dish for Easter breakfast one year, and our whole family loved the combination of bacon, eggs, noodles and cheese. Now I sometimes assemble this lasagna the night before and bake it in the morning for a terrific hassle-free brunch entree.

overnight pancakes

1 package (¼ ounce) active dry yeast

¼ cup warm water (110° to 115°)

4 cups all-purpose flour

2 tablespoons baking powder

2 teaspoons baking soda

2 teaspoons sugar

1 teaspoon salt

6 eggs

1 quart buttermilk

¼ cup vegetable oil

1 In a small bowl, dissolve yeast in water; let stand for 5 minutes. Meanwhile, in a large bowl, combine the dry ingredients. Beat eggs, buttermilk and oil; stir into dry ingredients just until moistened. Stir in yeast mixture. Cover and refrigerate for 8 hours or overnight.

2 To make pancakes, pour batter by ¼ cupfuls onto a greased hot griddle; turn when bubbles form on top of pancakes. Cook until second side is golden brown.

YIELD: ABOUT 2½ DOZEN

Lisa Sammons, Cut Bank, Montana

To ease the morning rush, I stir up this simple buttermilk batter ahead of time and refrigerate it overnight. In the morning, it's ready to go on the griddle. The fluffy, golden brown pancakes topped with fruit sauce or syrup are wonderful for Sunday brunch, busy weekdays…any time at all.

strawberry rhubarb coffee cake

Benita Thomas, Falcon, Colorado

We have a rhubarb patch, so I'm constantly looking for ways to use up my harvest. I've served this scrumptious coffee cake to people who say they don't like rhubarb, and they've always told me how much they enjoyed it.

2/3 cup sugar

1/3 cup cornstarch

2 cups chopped rhubarb

1 package (10 ounces) frozen sweetened sliced strawberries, thawed

2 tablespoons lemon juice

CAKE:

3 cups all-purpose flour

1 cup sugar

1 teaspoon baking powder

1/2 teaspoon baking soda

1 cup cold butter

2 eggs

1 cup buttermilk

1 teaspoon vanilla extract

TOPPING:

3/4 cup sugar

1/2 cup all-purpose flour

1/4 cup cold butter

1 In a saucepan, combine sugar and cornstarch; stir in rhubarb and strawberries. Bring to a boil over medium heat; cook for 2 minutes or until thickened. Remove from the heat; stir in lemon juice. Cool.

2 For cake, combine flour, sugar, baking powder and baking soda in a large bowl. Cut in butter until mixture resembles coarse crumbs. Beat the eggs, buttermilk and vanilla; stir into crumb mixture just until moistened. Spoon two-thirds of the batter into a greased 13-in. x 9-in. x 2-in. baking pan. Spoon cooled filling over batter. Top with remaining batter.

3 For topping, combine sugar and flour. Cut in butter until mixture resembles coarse crumbs; sprinkle over batter. Bake at 350° for 45-50 minutes or until golden brown. Cool on a wire rack.

YIELD: 12-15 SERVINGS

blueberry kuchen

1 1/2 cups all-purpose flour

3/4 cup sugar

2 teaspoons baking powder

1 1/2 teaspoons grated lemon peel

1/2 teaspoon ground nutmeg

1/4 teaspoon salt

2/3 cup milk

1/4 cup butter, melted

1 egg, beaten

1 teaspoon vanilla extract

2 cups fresh or frozen blueberries

TOPPING:

3/4 cup sugar

1/2 cup all-purpose flour

1/4 cup butter, melted

1 In a mixing bowl, combine the first six ingredients. Add the milk, butter, egg and vanilla. Beat for 2 minutes or until well blended. Pour into a greased 13-in. x 9-in. x 2-in. baking pan. Sprinkle with blueberries.

2 In a bowl, combine sugar and flour; add butter. Toss with a fork until crumbly; sprinkle over blueberries. Bake at 350° for 40 minutes or until lightly browned.

YIELD: 12 SERVINGS

Anne Krueger, Richmond, British Columbia

Our local peat bogs are known around the world for their beautiful

blueberries, and I'm always happy to take advantage of the bountiful crop.

This quick crumbly kuchen is one of my favorite blueberry recipes.

french toast casserole

1 loaf (10 ounces) French bread, cut into 1-inch cubes (10 cups)

8 eggs

3 cups milk

4 teaspoons sugar

1 teaspoon vanilla extract

¾ teaspoon salt, optional

TOPPING:

2 tablespoons butter, cubed

3 tablespoons sugar

2 teaspoons ground cinnamon

Maple syrup, optional

1 Place bread cubes in a greased 13-in. x 9-in. x 2-in. baking dish. In a mixing bowl, beat eggs, milk, sugar, vanilla and salt if desired. Pour over bread. Cover and refrigerate for 8 hours or overnight.

2 Remove from the refrigerator 30 minutes before baking. Dot with butter. Combine sugar and cinnamon; sprinkle over the top. Cover and bake at 350° for 45-50 minutes or until a knife inserted near the center comes out clean. Let stand for 5 minutes. Serve with syrup if desired.

YIELD: 12 SERVINGS

Sharyn Adams, Crawfordsville, Indiana

Cinnamon and sugar top this fuss-free dish that tastes just like French toast. Since you assemble it the previous night, you save time in the morning. Maple syrup makes the perfect accompaniment.

southwest sausage bake

Barbara Waddel, Lincoln, Nebraska

This layered tortilla dish is not only delicious, but it's also a real time-saver because it goes together the day before. The tomato slices on top provide an eye-catching touch of color. I like to serve this crowd-pleasing casserole with sour cream and salsa.

6 flour tortillas (10 inches), cut into ½-inch strips

4 cans (4 ounces *each*) chopped green chilies, drained

1 pound bulk pork sausage, cooked and drained

2 cups (8 ounces) shredded Monterey Jack cheese

10 eggs

½ cup milk

½ teaspoon *each* salt, garlic salt, onion salt, pepper and ground cumin

Paprika

2 medium tomatoes, sliced

Sour cream and salsa

1 In a greased 13-in. x 9-in. x 2-in. baking dish, layer half of the tortilla strips, chilies, sausage and cheese. Repeat layers. In a bowl, beat the eggs, milk and seasonings; pour over cheese. Sprinkle with paprika. Cover and refrigerate overnight.

2 Remove from the refrigerator 30 minutes before baking. Bake, uncovered, at 350° for 50 minutes. Arrange tomato slices over the top. Bake 10-15 minutes longer or until a knife inserted near the center comes out clean. Let stand for 10 minutes before cutting. Serve with sour cream and salsa.

YIELD: 12 SERVINGS

ham 'n' cheese strata

12 slices white bread, crusts removed

1 pound fully cooked ham, diced

2 cups (8 ounces) shredded cheddar cheese

6 eggs

3 cups milk

2 teaspoons Worcestershire sauce

1 teaspoon ground mustard

1/2 teaspoon salt

1/4 teaspoon pepper

Dash cayenne pepper

1/4 cup minced onion

1/4 cup minced green pepper

1/4 cup butter, melted

1 cup crushed cornflakes

1 Arrange six slices of bread in the bottom of a greased 13-in. x 9-in. x 2-in. baking dish. Top with ham and cheese. Cover with remaining bread. In a bowl, beat eggs, milk, Worcestershire sauce, mustard, salt, pepper and cayenne. Stir in onion and green pepper; pour over all. Cover and refrigerate overnight.

2 Remove from the refrigerator 30 minutes before baking. Pour butter over bread; sprinkle with cornflakes. Bake, uncovered, at 350° for 50-60 minutes or until a knife inserted near the center comes out clean. Let stand 10 minutes before serving.

YIELD: 8-10 SERVINGS

Marilyn Kroeker, Steinbach, Manitoba

My family wouldn't mind if I served them this dish every weekend! A hearty combination of popular breakfast ingredients, this layered casserole is a guaranteed crowd-pleaser at morning potlucks.

cocoa macaroon muffins

2 cups all-purpose flour

½ cup sugar

3 tablespoons baking cocoa

3 teaspoons baking powder

1 teaspoon salt

1 cup milk

1 egg

⅓ cup vegetable oil

1¼ cups flaked coconut, *divided*

¼ cup sweetened condensed milk

¼ teaspoon almond extract

1 In a bowl, combine flour, sugar, cocoa, baking powder and salt. Combine milk, egg and oil; mix well. Stir into dry ingredients just until moistened. Spoon 2 tablespoonfuls into 12 greased or paper-lined muffin cups.

2 Combine 1 cup coconut, condensed milk and extract; place 2 teaspoonfuls in the center of each cup (do not spread). Top with remaining batter; sprinkle with remaining coconut. Bake at 400° for 20-22 minutes or until a toothpick comes out clean. Cool for 5 minutes before removing from pan to a wire rack.

YIELD: 1 DOZEN

Carol Wilson, Rio Rancho, New Mexico

A longtime favorite that I've modified over the years, this recipe is wonderful for breakfast, as a snack or for dessert. I love chocolate in any form, and these mouth-watering muffins pair it with coconut for a yummy result. People especially like the surprise filling in the center.

citrus grove punch

Susan West, North Grafton, Massachusetts

Tangy and refreshing at any time of day, this sparkling punch blends traditional morning orange juice with grapefruit and lime juices and ginger ale. For a pretty presentation, add a citrus fruit garnish to each glass.

3 cups sugar

2 cups water

6 cups orange juice, chilled

6 cups grapefruit juice, chilled

1½ cups lime juice, chilled

1 liter ginger ale, chilled

In a saucepan, bring sugar and water to a boil; cook for 5 minutes. Cover and refrigerate until cool. Combine juices and sugar mixture; mix well. Just before serving, stir in ginger ale. Serve over ice.

YIELD: 6 QUARTS

quench the thirst of a crowd

If you're in charge of providing the beverages for a potluck, use these guidelines to estimate how much you'll need per person. Keep in mind that if you offer more than one of the following beverages, you'll need less per serving.

- Punch—1 cup
- Coffee—¾ cup
- Soft drinks—24 ounces
- Juice—24 ounces
- Tea—¾ cup
- Lemonade—24 ounces
- Bottled water—24 ounces

smoky bacon wraps

1 pound sliced bacon

1 package (16 ounces) miniature smoked sausage links

1 cup packed brown sugar

Cut each bacon strip in half widthwise. Wrap one piece of bacon around each sausage. Place in a foil-lined 15-in. x 10-in. x 1-in. baking pan. Sprinkle with brown sugar. Bake, uncovered, at 400° for 30-40 minutes or until bacon is crisp and sausage is heated through.

YIELD: ABOUT 3½ DOZEN

Cara Flora, Kokomo, Indiana

Requiring just three ingredients, these cute little sausage and bacon bites are a no-fuss breakfast dish. They have a sweet and salty taste that makes them great appetizers, too.

lemon poppy seed bread

1 box (18¼ ounces) white cake mix without pudding

1 package (3.4 ounces) instant lemon pudding mix

4 eggs

1 cup warm water

½ cup vegetable oil

4 teaspoons poppy seeds

1 In a mixing bowl, combine the cake and pudding mixes, eggs, water and oil; beat until well mixed. Fold in poppy seeds. Pour into two greased 9-in. x 5-in. x 3-in. loaf pans.

2 Bake at 350° for 35-40 minutes or until a toothpick inserted near the center comes out clean. Cool in pans for 10 minutes before removing to a wire rack.

YIELD: 2 LOAVES

Karen Dougherty, Freeport, Illinois

The days that I have extra time for baking are few and far between. That's why this extra-quick bread is one I turn to often. In about an hour, I have two luscious lemon loaves ready to slice and enjoy.

strawberry fruit dip

Lydia Graf, Norton, Ohio

I received this luscious recipe from my husband's cousin, and it's now a must-have dip whenever I'm serving a platter of fresh fruit. I simply combine sliced strawberries, sour cream, sugar and vanilla in the blender, then fold in whipped cream.

1 cup sliced fresh strawberries

¼ cup sour cream

1 tablespoon sugar

¼ teaspoon vanilla extract

½ cup heavy whipping cream

Assorted fresh fruit

In a blender, combine the strawberries, sour cream, sugar and vanilla. Cover and process until smooth. In a small mixing bowl, beat cream until stiff peaks form. Fold into strawberry mixture. Cover and refrigerate for at least 1 hour. Serve with fruit.

YIELD: 1½ CUPS

tangy fruit punch

1 can (46 ounces) pineapple juice

1 can (12 ounces) frozen orange juice concentrate, thawed

¾ cup lemonade concentrate

1 cup water, *divided*

½ cup sugar

2 large ripe bananas

1 package (20 ounces) frozen unsweetened whole strawberries, thawed

2 liters ginger ale, chilled

In a punch bowl or large container, combine pineapple juice, orange juice concentrate, lemonade concentrate, ½ cup water and sugar. Place bananas, strawberries and remaining water in a blender; cover and process until smooth. Stir into the juice mixture. Cover and refrigerate. Just before serving, stir in ginger ale.

YIELD: 25-30 SERVINGS (ABOUT 5 QUARTS)

Ann Cousin, New Braunfels, Texas

Many different fruit flavors mingle in this rosy refreshing punch. It's an especially nice beverage for a brunch because its versatile sweet-tart taste goes wonderfully with all kinds of foods, from scrambled eggs to sliced ham.

creamy hash brown bake

1 can (10¾ ounces) condensed cream of mushroom soup, undiluted

1 can (10¾ ounces) condensed cheddar cheese soup, undiluted

1 cup (8 ounces) sour cream

½ cup butter, softened

¼ cup chopped onion

½ teaspoon salt

1 package (28 ounces) frozen O'Brien hash brown potatoes

¾ cup crushed potato chips

In a large bowl, combine the soups, sour cream, butter, onion and salt. Add potatoes; mix well. Pour into a greased 13-in. x 9-in. x 2-in. baking dish. Sprinkle with potato chips. Bake, uncovered, at 350° for 55-60 minutes or until the potatoes are tender.

YIELD: 10-12 SERVINGS

Yvonna Nave, Lyons, Kansas

This cheesy casserole couldn't be much easier to prepare—I just mix ingredients together, then sprinkle crushed potato chips on top. The result is so rich and satisfying, some people enjoy this potato bake as a meatless main dish.

veggie-packed strata

Jennifer Unsell, Tuscaloosa, Alabama

People are always eager to try this deliciously different casserole featuring eggs and cheese. Baked in a springform pan, this strata catches folks' attention with colorful peppers, mushrooms, onion and other vegetables.

2 medium sweet red peppers, julienned

1 medium sweet yellow pepper, julienned

1 large red onion, sliced

3 garlic cloves, minced

3 tablespoons olive oil, *divided*

2 medium yellow summer squash, thinly sliced

2 medium zucchini, thinly sliced

½ pound fresh mushrooms, sliced

1 package (8 ounces) cream cheese, softened

¼ cup heavy whipping cream

2 teaspoons salt

1 teaspoon pepper

6 eggs

8 slices bread, cubed, *divided*

2 cups (8 ounces) shredded Swiss cheese

1 In a large skillet, saute the peppers, onion and garlic in 1 tablespoon oil until tender. Drain; pat dry and set aside. In the same skillet, saute yellow squash, zucchini and mushrooms in remaining oil until tender. Drain; pat dry and set aside.

2 In a large mixing bowl, beat the cream cheese, cream, salt and pepper until smooth. Beat in eggs. Stir in vegetables, half of the bread cubes and Swiss cheese. Arrange the remaining bread cubes in a greased 10-in. springform pan. Place on a baking sheet. Pour egg mixture into pan.

3 Bake, uncovered, at 325° for 60-70 minutes or until a knife inserted near the center comes out clean. Let stand for 10 minutes before serving. Run a knife around edge of pan to loosen; remove sides. Cut into wedges.

YIELD: 8-10 SERVINGS

almond fruit squares

2 tubes (8 ounces *each*) refrigerated crescent rolls

3 tablespoons sugar, *divided*

1 package (8 ounces) cream cheese, softened

1/3 cup almond paste

1/2 teaspoon almond extract

2 cups halved fresh strawberries

1 can (11 ounces) mandarin oranges, drained

1 cup fresh raspberries

1 cup halved green grapes

2 kiwifruit, peeled, quartered and sliced

1/2 cup apricot preserves, warmed

1/2 cup slivered almonds, toasted

1 Unroll crescent dough and separate into eight rectangles. Place in an ungreased 15-in. x 10-in. x 1-in. baking pan. Press onto bottom and up sides; seal seams and perforations. Sprinkle with 1 tablespoon sugar. Bake at 375° for 14-16 minutes or until golden brown. Cool.

2 In a mixing bowl, beat cream cheese, almond paste, extract and remaining sugar until smooth. Spread over crust. Top with fruit. Brush with preserves; sprinkle with almonds.

YIELD: 16 SERVINGS

Iola Egle, McCook, Nebraska

These sweet squares are easy to prepare, thanks to the refrigerated crescent roll dough that serves as the crust. With a layer of cream cheese, they can be served for breakfast or as a dessert any time of day.

raspberry cream cheese coffee cake

2¼ cups all-purpose flour

¾ cup sugar

¾ cup cold butter

½ teaspoon baking powder

½ teaspoon baking soda

½ teaspoon salt

¾ cup sour cream

1 egg, beaten

1½ teaspoons almond extract

FILLING:

1 package (8 ounces) cream cheese, softened

½ cup sugar

1 egg

½ cup raspberry jam

½ cup slivered almonds

1 In a large mixing bowl, combine flour and sugar; cut in butter until mixture is crumbly. Remove 1 cup and set aside. To the remaining crumb mixture, add baking powder, baking soda, salt, sour cream, egg and almond extract; mix well. Spread onto the bottom and 2 in. up the sides of a greased 9-in. springform pan.

2 For filling, combine cream cheese, sugar and egg in a small mixing bowl; beat well. Spoon over batter. Top with raspberry jam. Sprinkle with almonds and reserved crumb mixture.

3 Bake at 350° for 55-60 minutes. Cool on a wire rack for 15 minutes. Carefully run a knife around edge of pan to loosen. Remove sides of pan. Cool completely. Store in the refrigerator.

YIELD: 9-12 SERVINGS

Susan Litwiller, Medford, Oregon

Like a cross between a coffee cake and cheesecake, this treat is a decadent addition to morning buffets. Raspberry jam gives the filling ruby-red color. For extra appeal, garnish each slice with fresh raspberries.

one-dish wonders

200

222

Keep it simple—that's exactly what you can do for your next potluck, thanks to the no-fuss foods in this chapter. Each easy recipe requires just one bowl, one pan or one platter to prepare. You'll finish in a flash and have little cleanup when you're through.

Toss together Italian Bread Salad (p. 200) using a single bowl...or use a baking pan to assemble Nutty Peach Crisp (p. 222). These and other effortless dishes prove it's true—you don't need complicated cooking techniques to serve up a potluck sensation.

italian bread salad

Sandra Castillo, Sun Prairie, Wisconsin

With its delicious pizza flavor, this out-of-the-ordinary salad is a great choice for potlucks...and hearty enough to serve as a main dish on busy weeknights. If you like, cut a block of mozzarella into cubes rather than using shredded cheese.

1 prebaked Italian bread shell crust (14 ounces), cubed

1½ cups diced fresh tomatoes

½ cup thinly sliced fresh basil

½ cup Italian salad dressing, *divided*

7 cups ready-to-serve salad greens

1 small green pepper, julienned

1 cup sliced pepperoni

1 cup (4 ounces) shredded mozzarella cheese

½ cup grated Parmesan cheese

½ cup sliced ripe olives

In a large salad bowl, combine bread cubes, tomatoes, basil and ¼ cup salad dressing; let stand for 5 minutes. Add the salad greens, green pepper, pepperoni, mozzarella cheese, Parmesan cheese and olives. Add remaining salad dressing and toss to coat.

YIELD: 8-10 SERVINGS

maple baked beans

1 medium onion, chopped

1 to 2 tablespoons vegetable oil

3 cans (28 ounces *each*) baked beans

1½ teaspoons ground mustard

1 teaspoon garlic salt

¾ to 1 cup maple syrup

In a Dutch oven or large kettle, cook onion in oil until tender. Add the beans, mustard and garlic salt. Cook over medium heat until bubbly, stirring occasionally. Add maple syrup; heat through, stirring occasionally.

YIELD: 8-10 SERVINGS

Brenda Tetreault, Newport Center, Vermont

I came up with this recipe in a pinch after running out of baked beans at our oldest daughter's birthday party. I simply dressed up canned beans with maple syrup and a few other ingredients to produce this sweet, saucy version that tastes like homemade. They're so easy to prepare that I rarely make baked beans from scratch anymore.

almond celery bake

1 bunch celery, sliced (about 6 cups)

¾ cup shredded cheddar cheese

½ teaspoon paprika

⅛ teaspoon pepper

1 can (10¾ ounces) condensed cream of celery soup, undiluted

1 cup soft bread crumbs

½ cup slivered almonds

Place the celery in a greased 2-qt. baking dish. Sprinkle with cheese, paprika and pepper. Top with the soup. Sprinkle with bread crumbs. Cover and bake at 375° for 45 minutes. Uncover; sprinkle with the almonds. Bake 10-15 minutes longer or until golden brown.

YIELD: 10-12 SERVINGS

Judi Messina, Coeur d'Alene, Idaho

Whenever potluck guests sample this unusual casserole, they're surprised at how delicious celery can be. I combine it with cream soup, cheddar cheese, bread crumbs and crunchy almonds for a satisfying side dish.

southwestern salad

Carolyn Oler, Gilbert, Arizona

My mother gave me this recipe several years ago, and I've prepared it many times since for potlucks and parties. With pinto beans and cheese, the salad can nicely complement a meaty Mexican entree...or even be served as a main dish.

1 can (15 ounces) pinto beans, rinsed and drained

1 bunch green onions with tops, sliced

1 large tomato, seeded and chopped

1 avocado, chopped

1 bottle (8 ounces) Catalina salad dressing, *divided*

2 cups (8 ounces) shredded cheddar cheese

1 medium head lettuce, torn into bite-size pieces

4 cups corn chips

1 In a large salad bowl, toss together the beans, green onions, tomato, avocado and half of the Catalina dressing. Top with cheese and then lettuce. Refrigerate.

2 Just before serving, add corn chips to salad and toss. Pass the remaining dressing.

YIELD: 8-10 SERVINGS

keep an outdoor tablecloth in place

When your potluck is outside, the corners of the tablecloth can flutter and flap in the breeze. To prevent this, simply tie a basic overhand knot at each corner of the tablecloth.

You could also remove some stitches from the hem and slip coins, metal washers or curtain weights inside. Or, for an elegant touch, bunch the fabric at each corner and tie the bunches with ribbon, tucking fresh flowers or sprigs of herbs inside.

zesty vegetable dip

1 cup mayonnaise

1 cup (4 ounces) shredded sharp
  cheddar cheese

1/2 cup sour cream

1 envelope Italian salad
  dressing mix

1 tablespoon dried minced onion

1 tablespoon dried parsley flakes

1 tablespoon lemon juice

1 teaspoon Worcestershire sauce

Assorted raw vegetables

In a small bowl, combine the first eight ingredients until well blended. Cover and refrigerate for 2 hours. Serve with vegetables.

YIELD: 2 CUPS

Laura Mills, Liverpool, New York

There's an abundance of excellent cheeses made in our state, but sharp cheddar is my family's favorite. That variety jazzes up this popular dip, which Mom used to make for all of our family gatherings. Now I prepare it myself for get-togethers. It's so good, it even got my kids to eat their vegetables!

marinated veggie salad

1 pint cherry tomatoes, halved

1 medium zucchini, cubed

1 medium yellow summer squash, cubed

1 medium cucumber, cubed

1 *each* medium sweet yellow, red and green pepper, cut into 1-inch pieces

1 can (6 ounces) pitted ripe olives, drained

1 small red onion, chopped

1/2 to 3/4 cup Italian salad dressing

In a serving bowl, combine all ingredients. Cover and refrigerate overnight.

YIELD: 12 SERVINGS

Lynn Grate, South Bend, Indiana

I've sampled many different kinds of vegetable salads, but this is my hands-down favorite. I get compliments every time I serve it—no one guesses how easy it is to create. I combine the veggies and dressing the night before, then simply store the salad in the refrigerator until I'm ready to leave for the potluck.

easy rhubarb dessert

Mildred Mesick, Richmond, New York

A memorable dessert doesn't have to be difficult to prepare, as this taste-tempting treat proves. I take a few moments to slice the rhubarb, then put all of the ingredients in a baking pan and pop it in the oven. Vanilla ice cream makes the perfect finishing touch.

4 cups sliced fresh *or* frozen rhubarb

1 package (3 ounces) raspberry gelatin

1/3 cup sugar

1 package (18 1/4 ounces) yellow *or* white cake mix

1 cup water

1/3 cup butter, melted

Ice cream, optional

Place rhubarb in a greased 13-in. x 9-in. x 2-in. baking dish. Sprinkle with the gelatin, sugar and cake mix. Pour water evenly over dry ingredients; drizzle with butter. Bake at 350° for 1 hour or until rhubarb is tender. Serve with ice cream if desired.

YIELD: 16-20 SERVINGS

patchwork rice pilaf

4 celery ribs, chopped

2 large onions, chopped

4 medium carrots, chopped

1 large green pepper, chopped

¼ cup butter

2 medium tart red apples, chopped

2 cups sliced fresh mushrooms

2 packages (6.2 ounces *each*)
   fast-cooking long grain and
   wild rice mix

2 cans (10½ ounces *each*)
   condensed chicken broth,
   undiluted

1½ cups water

½ cup slivered almonds

1 In a large skillet or saucepan, saute the celery, onions, carrots and green pepper in butter until crisp-tender. Add the apples and mushrooms; saute for 2 minutes. Stir in the rice, contents of seasoning packets, broth and water; bring to a boil.

2 Reduce heat; cover and simmer according to rice package directions or until rice is tender and liquid is absorbed. Sprinkle with almonds.

YIELD: 12 SERVINGS

Brenda Scarbeary, Oelwein, Iowa

Colorful and versatile, this side dish goes well with a variety of meats and always disappears when I bring it to a potluck or picnic. Chopped apples make a pretty ruby-red addition and bring a subtle sweetness to the rice.

seven-fruit salad

1 can (29 ounces) sliced peaches, drained

2 cans (11 ounces *each*) mandarin oranges, drained

1 can (20 ounces) unsweetened pineapple chunks, drained

1 cup cherry pie filling

1 cup halved fresh strawberries

1 cup green grapes

½ cup fresh *or* frozen blueberries

In a large bowl, combine the peaches, oranges, pineapple and pie filling. Add the strawberries, grapes and blueberries; stir gently. Refrigerate leftovers.

YIELD: 10 SERVINGS

Martha Cutler, Willard, Missouri

I experimented with one of my grandmother's recipes and came up with this refreshing medley. Using convenient canned peaches and pineapple chunks means you don't have to spend a lot of time cutting before assembling the salad. For a change of pace, vary the fruit or add strawberry pie filling instead of cherry.

tangy pork barbecue

Carmine Walters, San Jose, California

A neighbor shared this flavorful pork recipe with me. The saucy barbecue was an instant hit with my family, so I knew it would be a great dish for get-togethers, too. We think the sandwiches are especially delicious served with French fries and coleslaw.

2 tablespoons butter

3 tablespoons all-purpose flour

1 bottle (28 ounces) ketchup

2 cups boiling water

¼ cup vinegar

¼ cup Worcestershire sauce

1 medium onion, chopped

1 garlic clove, minced

2 teaspoons chili powder

1 teaspoon salt, optional

1 teaspoon ground mustard

⅛ teaspoon cayenne pepper

1 boneless pork loin roast (3½ to 4 pounds)

12 sandwich buns, split

1 In a Dutch oven over medium heat, melt butter. Stir in flour until smooth. Add the next 10 ingredients; bring to a boil. Add roast. Reduce heat; cover and simmer for 3 hours or until meat is very tender.

2 Remove meat; shred with two forks or a pastry blender. Skim fat from cooking juices; return meat to juices and heat through. Serve with a slotted spoon on buns.

YIELD: 12 SERVINGS

tote food in a hot and cool way

Perfect for potlucks, insulated food carriers keep your food at the proper temperature during transport, so your hot or cold dishes will be ready to serve when you arrive at the potluck. Keep in mind that these carriers can maintain hot or cold temperatures only for a limited period of time. To ensure your food is safe to eat, follow the manufacturer's directions for the recommended maximum holding times.

pistachio mallow salad

1 carton (16 ounces) frozen whipped topping, thawed

1 package (3.4 ounces) instant pistachio pudding mix

6 to 7 drops green food coloring, optional

3 cups miniature marshmallows

1 can (20 ounces) crushed pineapple, undrained

1/2 cup chopped pistachios *or* walnuts

In a large bowl, combine whipped topping, pudding mix and food coloring if desired. Fold in the marshmallows and pineapple. Cover and refrigerate for at least 2 hours. Just before serving, sprinkle with nuts.

YIELD: 12 SERVINGS

Pattie Ann Forssberg, Logan, Kansas

This fluffy, not-too-sweet treat is easy to put together with whipped topping, pudding, mini marshmallows and pineapple. Just before setting the salad out on the buffet table, I sprinkle on pistachios or walnuts.

taco stovetop supper

2 pounds lean ground beef

2 cans (15½ ounces *each*) hot chili beans, undrained

2 cans (10 ounces *each*) diced tomatoes and green chilies, undrained

1 can (11½ ounces) picante V8 juice

1 can (11 ounces) Mexicorn, drained

2 envelopes taco seasoning

Optional garnishes: tortillas, shredded cheddar cheese, chopped onion, shredded lettuce *and/or* taco sauce

In a Dutch oven, cook beef over medium heat until no longer pink; drain. Stir in beans, tomatoes, V8 juice, corn and taco seasoning. Simmer, uncovered, for 15-20 minutes or until heated through. Garnish as desired.

YIELD: 10-12 SERVINGS

Barbara Inglis, Addy, Washington
Green chilies, Mexicorn and taco seasoning add south-of-the-border zip to this quick skillet dish. Potluck guests can spoon it onto tortillas, then top it off with shredded cheese, chopped onion and other garnishes.

oven cheese chowder

Martha Eastham, San Diego, California

Rich and creamy, this oven-baked chowder is loaded with chunks of zucchini, onion and other vegetables. It's a great way to use up fresh-picked garden produce but tastes wonderful any time of year. People like to sprinkle extra shredded Monterey Jack on top.

- ½ pound zucchini, cut into 1-inch chunks
- 2 medium onions, chopped
- 1 can (15 ounces) garbanzo beans, rinsed and drained
- 1 can (14½ ounces) diced tomatoes with liquid
- 1 can (11 ounces) Mexicorn, drained
- 1 can (14½ ounces) chicken broth
- 2 teaspoons salt
- ¼ teaspoon pepper
- 1 garlic clove, minced
- 1 teaspoon dried basil
- 1 bay leaf
- 1 cup (4 ounces) shredded Monterey Jack cheese
- 1 cup grated Romano cheese
- 1½ cups half-and-half cream
- Additional Monterey Jack cheese, optional

1 In a 3-qt. baking dish, combine the first 11 ingredients. Cover and bake at 400° for 1 hour, stirring once.

2 Stir in the cheeses and cream. Bake, uncovered, for 10 minutes. Remove bay leaf. Top with additional Monterey Jack if desired.

YIELD: 10-12 SERVINGS (3 QUARTS)

italian sausage and peppers

3 pounds Italian sausage links, cut into ¾-inch slices

4 medium green peppers, cut into thin strips

1 medium onion, thinly sliced and quartered

1 tablespoon butter

1 tablespoon olive oil

3 tablespoons chicken broth

6 plum tomatoes, coarsely chopped

1 tablespoon minced fresh parsley

½ teaspoon salt

¼ teaspoon pepper

½ teaspoon lemon juice

In a Dutch oven, cook the sausage over medium heat until no longer pink; drain. Add the remaining ingredients. Cover and cook for 30 minutes or until vegetables are tender, stirring occasionally. Serve with a slotted spoon.

YIELD: 12 SERVINGS

Jeanne Corsi, Arnold, Pennsylvania

My sister was hosting a birthday party and asked me to bring a sausage-and-pepper dish. I'd never made one before, so I tried altering a braised pepper recipe. Now family members often request this main course.

hearty chicken vegetable soup

1 roasting chicken (about 5 pounds), cut up and skin removed

2 celery ribs, sliced

1 large onion, chopped

2½ quarts water

1 can (14½ ounces) stewed tomatoes

4 medium carrots, sliced

2 medium potatoes, peeled and cubed

1 medium turnip, peeled and cubed

2 tablespoons chicken bouillon granules

½ teaspoon minced fresh parsley

¾ teaspoon *each* dried basil, oregano and tarragon

¾ teaspoon salt

¾ teaspoon pepper

½ teaspoon garlic powder

2 cups broccoli florets

2 cups frozen peas, optional

1 Place the chicken, celery, onion and water in a Dutch oven or soup kettle; bring to a boil. Skim fat. Reduce heat; cover and simmer for 1½ to 2 hours or until chicken is tender. Remove chicken; cool. Remove meat from bones and cut into bite-size pieces; return to pan.

2 Add tomatoes, carrots, potatoes, turnip, bouillon and seasonings; bring to a boil. Reduce heat; cover and simmer for 20 minutes. Add broccoli and peas if desired; simmer 15-20 minutes longer or until vegetables are tender.

YIELD: 16 SERVINGS (ABOUT 4 QUARTS)

Bertha Vogt, Tribune, Kansas

I experimented with different ingredients to create a chicken-vegetable soup, and this is the recipe I came up with. Family and friends often request it for potlucks. Any leftovers are wonderful reheated for lunch the next day.

taco dip platter

Marieann Johansen, Desert Hot Springs, California

To make this easy-as-can-be appetizer, you simply layer refried beans, salsa, cheeses and other favorite taco ingredients on a serving platter. All that's left to do is set out a big basket of tortilla chips, and people will dig right in.

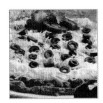

1 can (15 ounces) refried beans

1 cup chunky salsa

1 cup guacamole

2 cups (16 ounces) sour cream

1 can (4 ounces) chopped green chilies

1 can (2¼ ounces) sliced ripe olives, drained

½ cup finely shredded cheddar cheese

½ cup finely shredded Monterey Jack cheese

Tortilla chips

Spread beans on a 12-in. serving plate. Layer salsa, guacamole and sour cream over beans, leaving 1 in. uncovered around edge of each layer. Sprinkle with chilies, olives and cheeses. Refrigerate until ready to serve. Serve with tortilla chips.

YIELD: 16-20 SERVINGS

nutty peach crisp

1 can (29 ounces) sliced peaches,
  undrained

1 package (18¼ ounces) yellow *or*
  butter pecan cake mix

½ cup butter, melted

1 cup flaked coconut

1 cup chopped pecans

1 Arrange peaches in an ungreased 13-in. x 9-in. x 2-in. baking dish.
  Sprinkle dry cake mix over top. Drizzle with butter; sprinkle with
  coconut and pecans.

2 Bake at 325° for 55-60 minutes or until golden brown. Let stand for
  15 minutes. Serve warm or cold.

YIELD: 12-15 SERVINGS

Nancy Carpenter, Sidney, Montana

A co-worker brought this easy, delicious dessert to work, and I couldn't resist
asking for the recipe. A moist bottom layer made with canned peaches and
boxed cake mix is covered with a lovely golden topping of coconut and
pecans. It's especially good served warm with vanilla ice cream.

double chip bars

½ cup butter

1½ cups graham cracker crumbs
(about 24 squares)

1 can (14 ounces) sweetened
condensed milk

2 cups semisweet chocolate chips

1 cup peanut butter chips

1 Place butter in a 13-in. x 9-in. x 2-in. baking pan; place in a 350° oven until melted. Remove from the oven. Sprinkle the cracker crumbs evenly over butter.

2 Pour milk evenly over crumbs. Sprinkle with chips; press down firmly. Bake at 350° for 25-30 minutes or until golden brown. Cool on a wire rack before cutting.

YIELD: 3 DOZEN

Victoria Lowe, Lititz, Pennsylvania

Adults and children alike enjoy munching these sweet treats that feature the popular combination of chocolate and peanut butter. The bars go together so quickly, I can whip up a batch on even the most hectic days.

festive favorites

230

234

At holiday time or for special celebrations, potlucks take on a festive air. Let your meal contributions reflect that merry spirit by sharing the seasonal and event-themed recipes featured in this chapter.

You'll find Christmas Glow Punch (p. 230) as a cheery beverage for December…Pumpkin-Pecan Cake Roll (p. 234) as a delightful fall dessert…and much more. Whichever timely foods you choose, they'll rise to the occasion.

vegetable wreath with dip

Edna Hoffman, Hebron, Indiana

Vegetables and dip are a mainstay at most holiday get-togethers. I like to dress up this appetizer by cutting vegetables into festive shapes and arranging them as a wreath. It's a nice conversation piece.

1 package (8 ounces) cream cheese, softened

¼ cup mayonnaise

½ teaspoon chili powder

½ teaspoon dill weed

¼ teaspoon garlic powder

¼ cup sliced green onions

¼ cup chopped ripe olives, well drained

4 cups broccoli florets

1 medium green pepper, cut into strips

8 cherry tomatoes

1 medium jicama *or* turnip, peeled and sliced

1 medium sweet red pepper

1 In a small mixing bowl, combine the first five ingredients; mix well. Stir in onions and olives. Cover and refrigerate for at least 2 hours.

2 Transfer dip to a serving bowl; place in the center of a 12-in. round serving plate. Arrange broccoli, green pepper and tomatoes in a wreath shape around dip. Using a small star cookie cutter, cut out stars from jicama slices; place over wreath. Cut red pepper into five pieces that form the shape of a bow; position on wreath.

YIELD: 12 SERVINGS

jingle bell spread

2 packages (8 ounces *each*) cream cheese, softened

½ cup mayonnaise *or* salad dressing

⅓ cup grated Parmesan cheese

10 bacon strips, cooked and crumbled

¼ cup sliced green onions

½ cup minced fresh parsley

1 jar (2 ounces) diced pimientos, drained

Sweet red pepper strips, optional

Assorted crackers

1 In a mixing bowl, beat cream cheese until smooth. Stir in mayonnaise, Parmesan cheese, bacon and onions. Drop by spoonfuls onto a serving platter in the shape of a bell; carefully spread with an icing knife to fill in the bell.

2 Sprinkle bell with parsley and pimientos. If desired, add red pepper strips across bell as shown in photo. Serve with crackers.

YIELD: 3 CUPS

Karen Balistrieri, Oconomowoc, Wisconsin

No need to ring this "dinner bell" to summon your guests—the sight of it's enough to make people come running! The creamy spread gets a festive look from red pepper, pimientos and parsley on top. If you like, you can mold the mixture into a Christmas tree, star, candy cane or other simple holiday shape.

poinsettia cookies

1 cup butter, softened

1 cup confectioners' sugar

1 egg

1½ teaspoons almond extract

1 teaspoon vanilla extract

2½ cups all-purpose flour

1 teaspoon salt

Red decorator's sugar

Red and green candied cherries, quartered

1 In a mixing bowl, cream butter and sugar. Add egg and extracts; mix well. Combine flour and salt; gradually add to creamed mixture. Divide dough in half; wrap in plastic wrap. Chill overnight or until firm.

2 On a lightly floured surface, roll out one portion of dough to a 12-in. x 10-in. rectangle approximately ⅛-in. thick. Cut into 2-in. squares. In each square, make 1-in. slits in each corner. Bring every other corner up into center to form a pinwheel; press lightly. Sprinkle cookies with red sugar and press a candied cherry piece into the center of each.

3 Place 1 in. apart on ungreased baking sheets. Bake at 350° for 8-10 minutes. Cool 1-2 minutes before removing to a wire rack.

YIELD: ABOUT 4 DOZEN

Helen Burch, Jamestown, New York

To make a basic butter cookie recipe look special for the season, I formed the dough into pretty poinsettias—no cookie cutters required. Candied cherry pieces and a sprinkling of red decorator's sugar give these sweet almond-flavored treats Christmas color.

christmas glow punch

Marge Hodel, Roanoke, Illinois

With a merry crimson color, this sweet tropical beverage always shines on a holiday buffet table. Let the punch base chill in the refrigerator, then add the ginger ale and raspberry sherbet just before serving.

4½ cups tropical punch

1 cup cranberry juice

1 can (6 ounces) pineapple juice

⅓ cup lemon juice

2 to 3 cups chilled ginger ale

1 pint raspberry sherbet

In a 2-qt. container, combine the punch and juices. Cover and refrigerate until chilled. Just before serving, transfer to a small punch bowl. Stir in ginger ale; top with scoops of sherbet.

YIELD: ABOUT 2 QUARTS

make guests merry with a peppermint stick container

Filled with silverware or flowers, a peppermint stick container is a fun addition to a Christmas buffet. To create one, stand a clean empty aluminum can on the table and place a rubber band around the center. Tuck wrapped peppermint sticks (that are taller than the can) behind the band, adding enough to hide the can.

If you like, trim the wrappers at the bottom of the sticks first so the ends will sit flat on the table. To finish, hide the rubber band with a decorative ribbon, then fill your container and place it on the table.

chocolate mint creams

1 cup butter, softened

1½ cups confectioners' sugar

2 squares (1 ounce *each*) unsweetened chocolate, melted and cooled

1 egg

1 teaspoon vanilla extract

2½ cups all-purpose flour

1 teaspoon baking soda

1 teaspoon cream of tartar

¼ teaspoon salt

FROSTING:

¼ cup butter, softened

2 cups confectioners' sugar

2 tablespoons milk

½ teaspoon peppermint extract

Green food coloring, optional

1 In a large mixing bowl, cream butter and confectioners' sugar. Add the chocolate, egg and vanilla; mix well. Combine the dry ingredients; gradually add to creamed mixture, beating well. Shape dough into a 2-in.-diameter roll; wrap in plastic wrap. Refrigerate for 1 hour or until firm.

2 Unwrap dough and cut into ⅛-in. slices. Place 2 in. apart on ungreased baking sheets. Bake at 400° for 7-8 minutes or until edges are firm. Remove to wire racks to cool. In a small mixing bowl, combine frosting ingredients. Tint with green food coloring if desired. Frost cookies. Store in airtight containers.

YIELD: ABOUT 6 DOZEN

Beverly Fehner, Gladstone, Missouri

With the ever-popular combination of chocolate and peppermint, this recipe from an old family friend is always high on everyone's cookie request list. I make at least six batches each year for Noel nibbling.

christmas fruit salad

3 egg yolks, beaten

3 tablespoons water

3 tablespoons vinegar

1/2 teaspoon salt

2 cups heavy whipping cream, whipped

3 cups miniature marshmallows

2 cups halved green grapes

1 can (20 ounces) pineapple tidbits, drained

1 can (11 ounces) mandarin oranges, drained

1 jar (10 ounces) red maraschino cherries, drained and sliced

1 cup chopped pecans

3 tablespoons lemon juice

1 In a large saucepan, combine egg yolks, water, vinegar and salt. Cook over medium heat, stirring constantly, until mixture thickens and reaches 160°. Remove from the heat and cool; fold in whipped cream.

2 In a large bowl, combine remaining ingredients. Add dressing; toss to coat. Cover and refrigerate 24 hours.

YIELD: 12-14 SERVINGS

Ina Vickers, Dumas, Arkansas

It was at one of the first holidays I spent with my husband's family that I first tasted this fluffy medley of fruit, marshmallows and chopped pecans. My mother-in-law shared the recipe, which offers make-ahead convenience. Now I often prepare this refreshing salad for special occasions, and it's a mainstay at the potlucks we have at work.

alphabetical recipe index

Refer to this index for a complete alphabetical listing of all the recipes in this book.

Metric Equivalents

VOLUME

IMPERIAL	METRIC
⅛ teaspoon	0.5 milliliter
¼ teaspoon	1 milliliter
½ teaspoon	2 milliliters
1 teaspoon	5 milliliters
1 tablespoon (½ fluid ounce)	1 tablespoon (15 milliliters)*
¼ cup (2 fluid ounces)	2 tablespoons (50 milliliters)
⅓ cup (3 fluid ounces)	¼ cup (75 milliliters)
½ cup (4 fluid ounces)	⅓ cup (125 milliliters)
¾ cup (6 fluid ounces)	¾ cup (200 milliliters)
1 cup (8 fluid ounces)	1 cup (250 milliliters)
1 pint (16 fluid ounces)	500 milliliters
1 quart (32 fluid ounces)	1 liter minus 3 tablespoons

The Australian tablespoon is 20 milliliters, but the difference is negligible in most recipes.

TEMPERATURE

IMPERIAL	METRIC
0°F (freezer temperature)	minus 18°C
32°F (temperature water freezes)	0°C
180°F (temperature water simmers)*	82°C
212°F (temperature water boils)*	100°C
250°F (low oven temperature)	120°C
350°F (moderate oven temperature)	180°C
425°F (hot oven temperature)	220°C
500°F (very hot oven temperature)	260°C

At sea level

WEIGHT

IMPERIAL	METRIC
¼ ounce	7 grams
½ ounce	15 grams
¾ ounce	20 grams
1 ounce	30 grams
6 ounces	170 grams
8 ounces (½ pound)	225 grams
12 ounces (¾ pound)	340 grams
16 ounces (1 pound)	450 grams
35 ounces (2 ¼ pounds)	1 kilogram

BAKING PAN SIZES

IMPERIAL	METRIC
8 x 1½-inch round cake pan	20 x 5-centimeter cake tin
9 x 1½-inch round cake pan	23 x 5-centimeter cake tin
11 x 7 x 1½-inch baking pan	28 x 18 x 4-centimeter baking tin
13 x 9 x 2-inch baking pan	30 x 20 x 3-centimeter baking tin
15 x 10 x 1-inch baking pan (jelly-roll pan)	38 x 25 x 2.5-centimeter baking tin (Swiss-roll tin)
9 x 5 x 3-inch loaf pan	25 x 7.5-centimeter loaf tin in Canada
	19 x 12 x 9-centimeter loaf tin in Australia
9-inch pie plate	23 x 3-centimeter pie plate
7- or 8-inch springform pan or loose-bottom tin	20-centimeter springform tin
10-inch tube or Bundt pan	26-centimeter (15-cup capacity) ring tin

NOTE: *Pan sizes vary between manufacturers, so use this list as an approximate guide only. Always use the nearest equivalent available.*

LENGTH

IMPERIAL	METRIC
½ inch	12 millimeters
1 inch	2.5 centimeters
6 inches	15 centimeters
12 inches (1 foot)	30 centimeters